THE
SUCCESS FACTOR

TED BAGLEY

Copyright © 2023 Ted Bagley.

All rights reserved. No part of this book may be reproduced, stored, or transmitted by any means—whether auditory, graphic, mechanical, or electronic—without written permission of both publisher and author, except in the case of brief excerpts used in critical articles and reviews. Unauthorized reproduction of any part of this work is illegal and is punishable by law.

ISBN: 979-8-88640-734-1 (sc)
ISBN: 979-8-88640-735-8 (hc)
ISBN: 979-8-88640-736-5 (e)

Because of the dynamic nature of the Internet, any web addresses or links contained in this book may have changed since publication and may no longer be valid. The views expressed in this work are solely those of the author and do not necessarily reflect the views of the publisher, and the publisher hereby disclaims any responsibility for them.

One Galleria Blvd., Suite 1900, Metairie, LA 70001
1-888-421-2397

"As for courage and will, we cannot measure how much of each lies within us; we can only trust there will be sufficient enough to carry through trials which may lie ahead".

—Andre Norton

CONTENTS

Acknowledgment vii
Abstract..ix
Preface xvii

Chapter 1   Generational Conflict..1
Chapter 2   Reading the Environment..................................10
Chapter 3   The Successful Beginning.................................20
Chapter 4   The Interview Process.......................................26
Chapter 5   Arrival at the New Location..............................41
Chapter 6   Understanding the Culture................................43
Chapter 7   Understanding what is Expected.......................45
Chapter 8   Things that are Career Boosters........................50
Chapter 9   The Value of Mentoring/Coaching 53
Chapter 10   Personal Branding...57

Summary 61
A Final Note 67
About the Author 71
Notable Quotes 73
References 75

ACKNOWLEDGMENT

As an Executive responsible for recruiting and hiring some of the best minds available from universities across the nation, I feel it necessary to help new entrants to the work force see clearly what they are facing in the aggressive and competitive world of Corporate America. A good start doesn't guarantee a successful finish, but a poor start could certainly place a career in an early coma.

I wrote this book because I have observed a disturbing trend of senior workers leaving the workforce in significant numbers at a time when younger generations are getting their sea legs and entering the stormy waters of corporate America. A loss of this intellectual capital without a plan to harness a portion of it, represents a significant risk to technical, medical, financial and legal superiority in this country. Knowledge and education are the key elements of any successful endeavor.

I didn't have anyone to share with me what I am about to share with you in these pages. I didn't have a mentor. I wasn't someone's protégé. My advice and information are to be shared with others who could benefit. The more education you have about your career direction prevents you from stepping into career limiting holes that are difficult to get out of once you have fallen in. You may be successful in digging out, but the energy and time taken to do so could derail your career.

I would like to take the time to thank the many workers who supported me with both written material and time in preparing this work. It is vital that the readers understand the political, structural and competitive challenges that awaits new entries into the world of work. Hopefully, this information will help in the early identification and *understanding of* career direction as applicants navigate the treacherous waters of Corporate America.

This work will become your handbook to success. It will give you the confidence and courage to carry your game to another level. Tell me what you think after exploring "**The Success Factors**"

ABSTRACT

Introduction

> *"A good name is more desirable than great riches;*
> *To be esteemed is better than silver or gold."*
>
> —Proverbs 22:1

The purpose of this work titled "<u>*Winning in the Corporate World*</u>" is to increase the successful integration of new entrants into an ever increasing diverse and competitive work environment. This book will not only deal with getting the job through proper etiquette, interviewing, pre and post job acceptance, but also the political view of keeping it in highly competitive environment. In these environments where significant generational conflict is becoming more the rule verses the exception, the winning equation is becoming increasingly challenging. For the first time in modern history, there are <u>***four generations***</u> of workers operating in the same corporate space with a fifth waiting in the wings. I will cover how these generations influence the corporate landscape today.

In a very short period of time, employers, a business associate, co-workers and community leaders will "check you out"—the way you dress; the way you walk; the way you express yourself; your facial expressions; the way you present yourself. Your body language speaks volumes about who you are.

Considering these premises, they begin forming an opinion about your personal brand based on that first impression. You will hear me speak a lot about your **personal brand** in these pages. That instant opinion could determine whether you get an opportunity, a promotion, or whether you remain satisfied with the status quo. Unfortunately, behaviors are driven by perceptions. The more knowledge gained, the more behavior is shaped. These few but sincere words ring so true in the direction that we seek both personally and from a career perspective. <u>**These revealing words ring so true in our lives and careers. OR These revealing words ring so true in our personal and professional lives OR These revealing words ring so true in our personal lives and occupations.**</u>

What you say, the quality of your work, promptness of your actions; your dependability, your can do attitude, your presentation style, your facial expressions, and body language all contribute to who you are in the eyes of those around you. It's your personal brand." Individuals are quick to judge you <u>*based*</u> on what they see or perceive, not on what they know.

<u>*Individuals are quick to judge you on what they see or perceive, not on What they know.*</u> Deleted the word "based"

The Six Personal Marketing tools that this book will explore are:

- *Persona..........Your personality, your personal* <u>**Brand.**</u> *What you put forth for others to see. How others form their opinions.*
- *Packaging.......Your background and experience. These are the tools in your tool box that place on display the competencies that others will rate you on.*
- *Positioning......Jobs and network/connections. In order to succeed in this world, others must be involved in your journey.*

- *Presentation......How you present yourself. This includes dress, oral and written presentation.*
- *Promotion.......Growth and development. Developing your skill set beyond your current position. Pushing the envelope beyond your comfort level,*
- *Passion...........Emotion and conviction. That extra edge that pushes you to the next level of performance.*

Your personality and behavior are more than half the battle. Many individuals never have their career truly realize its full potential, primarily because of how they behave toward others in a team environment. Next comes the packaging of your competencies which includes but are not limited to first impression, basic knowledge, appearance, and perceptions. Now consider the idea of positioning yourself for success through mentorships, networking, cross functional assignments and constant skill upgrade. What about your presentation skills? These skills tend to be one of the major derailleurs of new entrants into the workforce. This is primarily the result of lack of preparation, confidence and presence. Any growth in the early stages of the career is affected greatly by successfully navigating these key premises. Finally, without emotional conviction and passion, a career is doomed to mediocrity.

I personally don't agree with the often quoted Woody Allen who said, "80 percent of success is showing up". Though there is much to be said about presence, it's the quality of the presence that tends to move mountains and level rough places. If you are a Hollywood star or a billionaire, then maybe there is application but most of us don't fit these elite categories. I agree that new and innovative technologies and markets are pushing us to the brink of our talent pool capabilities as we all seek that very illusive competitive advantage. The bottom line is, "we have to do more than just show up". Trail blazers of the past fashioned new pathways to new inventions. They didn't settle for the status quo.

Many companies readily _identify_ key talent but equally as many have struggled to maintain it in markets where talent pools are shrinking.

New generation talent pools are very mobile and often sell their competencies to the highest bidder. Staff development, maturation and retention play a major role in ensuring a stable and talented work environment. Many companies carry on bidding wars for key talent in critical skill areas. They are willing to spend what they must to get who they want, even at above market compensation. The problem that is created by bringing individuals into an environment above the market value for the position is evident.

As a result of these increasing missteps, companies are struggling to get a comparable return on that investment, if in fact they are able to retain the talent for any length of time. Additionally, it makes future compensation growth opportunities difficult as he/she seeks to enhance their salary base.

Why do you care? There are many books on the market covering effective recruiting, resume writing and proper professional dress but very few on what happens inside the corporate community and how to continually progress beyond the initial hire date. Many companies have varying cultures but the majority of the key initiatives remain the same. Retention of key talent, adequate compensation, fair and progressive environments, competent and passionate leaders, and a flexible and diverse mindset, tend to permeate most corporate institutions. Those who are able to navigate these waters are the most sought after candidates.

A corporate culture is defined in many different ways. Some say it is the social infrastructure or architecture of an organization which is translated through its policies, procedures, laws and regulations. Others say it's the social genre of the organization - what employees do outside their normal responsibilities and *how people-centric programs are handled*. Whatever form the environment of an organization takes, it's the responsibility of the new entrant to evaluate it. <u>What are the growth possibilities and how will the entrant's personality, brand, and social style match the new environment?</u> "related to his or her growth possibilities and how his/her personality, social style and brand will match with the new environment"

Across many industries, there remains a high attrition rate for new entrants. The primary cause is the lack of preparation in navigating the ambiguous, competitive, challenging, and changing undercurrents they will face. . No longer can individuals just specialize in a certain core competency, they must multi-task and build relationships with cultures they have no prior relationships with or minimal knowledge of. Additionally, without project integration skills or multi degrees, many students from less prestigious colleges and universities have a difficult time competing with students coming from the top MBA schools for a dwindling pool of key opportunities.

Your personal brand and competencies, no matter how they are packaged, can be the deciding factor between a highly successful career and a floundering run of mid-level jobs. Companies are seeking individuals who are comfortable in their own skins, excellent decision makers and those who can operate within the walls of the board room as well as having credible relationships at lower levels of the organization. **Good** is no longer good enough. The great past coach of the Green Bay Packers, Vince Lombardi, once said:

> *"Winning is not a sometime thing; it's an all-the-time thing. You don't win once in a while; you don't do things right once in a while, you do them right all the time. Winning is a habit. Unfortunately, so is losing." "There is no room for second place. There is only one place in my game and that is first place. I have finished second twice in my time at Green Bay and I don't ever want to finish second again. There is a second place bowl game; but it is a game for losers played by losers. It is and always has been an American zeal to be first in anything we do and to win and win and win. "Every time a football player goes out to apply his trade he's got to play from the ground up – from*

the soles of his feet right up to his head. Every inch of him has to play.

"Some guys play with their heads. That's OK. You've got to be smart to be No. 1 in any business. But more important, you've got to play with your heart, with every fiber of your body. If you're lucky enough to find a guy who uses his head and a lot of heart, he's never going to come off the field second."

"Running a football team is no different from running any other kind of organization — an army, a political party, a business. The principles are the same. The object is to win — to beat the other guy. Maybe that sounds hard or cruel. I don't think it is." "It's a reality of life that men are competitive and the most competitive games draw the most competitive men. That's why they're there — to compete. They know the rules and the objectives when they get in the game. The objective is to win — fairly, squarely, decently, by the rules — but to win."

"And in truth, I've never known a man worth his salt who in the long run, deep down in his heart, didn't appreciate the grind, the discipline. There is something in good men that really yearns for, needs, discipline and the harsh reality of head-to-head combat.

I don't say these things because I believe in the 'brute' nature of man or that men must be brutalized to be combative. I believe in God, and I believe in human decency. But I firmly believe that any man's finest hour — his greatest fulfillment to all he holds dear — is that moment when he has worked his heart out in a good cause and lies exhausted on the field of battle — victorious."

This winning that Vince talks about is applied in our everyday lives and occupations. That's the dedication, the passion that will push us to reach heights that even we sometimes didn't think we were capable of. We owe it to our employers, our team members and most of all to ourselves, to be emotionally tied to extracting the best competency DNA, with every fiber of our being. Working hard, smart, and with conviction almost guarantees success. But, remember, success is found before work only in the dictionary.

Companies are seeking the best available talent and will not hesitate to attract the talent from wherever it's found, including attracting it from the competition. The top recruiters tend to target markets where certain types of competencies are found. They are not afraid to use the direct approach of setting up shop in the back yard of key competitors and targeting their best and brightest resources. In fact, that is preferable because it decreases training cost and lower the time for individuals to get up to speed on familiar product lines, processes and deliveries. Coming in with the prerequisite skills is increasingly desired by leading edge companies. Many companies rotate from having sixty percent make (promotion from within) to sixty percent buy (attracting the skill from outside) on any given year. There is something to be said for companies who periodically look to the outside to bring in new ideas which support the long term growth of the institution. These new entrants bring variety, freshness and high energy to a sometimes stagnant culture.

As new entrants to the workforce forge their individual path to a career of opportunity and challenge, they will face the old demon called perception. As competitive as we can be, we tend to form opinions quickly. Hasty opinions send us on a journey of false assumptions and innuendoes that more often than not, cheat us of the rich relationship that "COULD HAVE BEEN". Once we read someone incorrectly, we tend to react to them based on the incorrect assumption and both the giver and receiver of the action is short-changed in the process.

Assumptions are perceived facts without foundation. Foundations are structures that support a strong edifice. Weak or lack of correct material and information generally leads to a crumbling foundation. Removing assumptions takes time and effort on the part of the individual affected. A misplaced assumption can be career limiting if facts are not quickly added to make the perception valid. Believe it or not, in your career you will deal more with perception than fact as it relates to human analysis. The quicker we transform perception to fact-based learning, the richer our experiences will be.

Conclusion: An individual who speaks multi-languages, has an impressive resume; communicates well; possess project management skills; displays exceptional role modeling tendencies; embraces change management; fosters multiculturalism; and displays a winning personality, will emerge as a future key leader in any progressive organization that is quick to embrace change. Understanding corporate politics and the global nature of most dynamic organizations will be paramount to ultimately solving the issues of **"navigating"** in a more challenging and globally competitive workplace.

PREFACE

This work has as its primary purpose, the educating of those entering the work place for the first time. It also includes those who change jobs, and who are lost in the workplace having no sense of direction or comprehension of what success looks like. Many are caught in a survival whirlpool where most of their energies are spent on their heels in a defensive mode without a clue of how to change their trajectory. Many are caught in the "*what*" of their careers instead of the "*why*" and "*how*". It is my desire to have you use this work as reference material on your personal journey as you continually climb the ladder to ultimate success.

To its conclusion, this book will address the current work environment of multi-culture; multi-generation; multi-skill; multi-tasking; emerging-markets; flex work schedules; opportunity mobility, and leading edge learning. Skills needed to succeed in this versatile world of careers are excellent collaboration; negotiation and communication skills; Project management; technological expertise including effective use of social networks; accounting 101; math and science aptitude; group and team leadership competencies. It may seem like a lot but no matter your expertise, you will have to use many of these listed competencies to be considered a part of the "Key to Retain" resource base.

Quoting from one of my favorite poets, Maya Angelou, "I've learned that people will forget what you said, people will forget what you did, but people will never forget how you made them feel." **She goes on to say,** "I've learned that you shouldn't go through life with a catcher's mitt on both hands; you need to be able to throw something back. This happens to be a baseball cliché' which get to the core of the learning process. You receive information and you give some of it back as part of the communication process.

It is my hope that after reading these navigating tools, you will feel this work has helped you in some way and that you have the catcher's mitt on just one hand. This work hopefully represents the ball that you will be thrown to someone else to get them started in the right direction. Passing the ball is the responsibility of anyone participating in the game of working to live.

As previously mentioned, what makes this work different from the many books and white papers currently in circulation is its focus on you the person and not simply starting a career but how to understand those things affecting it and you in both positive and negative ways. This work addresses not only the strategic and technical parts of obtaining a career position but it will also address the new and growing phenomenon of the generations and particularly the renaissance of the more tenured workers. The bureau of Labor Statistics predicts that 43 percent of the workforce operating between the years 2004 and 2012 will be eligible to retire in the next 10 years.

I question whether big and small businesses are in any way prepared to handle this brain drain and potential loss of vital intellectual capital and experience. As the Baby Boomer generation matures, the impact what is sure to be massive change which will require leaders to deploy change management tools at a level never experienced before.

Places like fast food establishments, banks and hospitals are quickly realizing the value of more experienced workers. They are less costly, more dependable with great interpersonal and customer service skills. They are thriving in service industries where technical and social networking skills are not predominant. Newer generations, if open minded, can learn from the competencies of the generations before them as each make up the core of industrial resources in today's work environment. Having four generations under one roof for the first time is not a temporary phenomenon. Unfortunately, the economy will not regain its momentum very quickly causing retirees to rethink their retirement strategies and remain in the workplace for extended periods.

CHAPTER I

GENERATIONAL CONFLICT

> *"Struggle is a never ending process. Freedom is never really won, you earn it and win it in every generation."*
>
> —*Coretta Scott King*

The generational melting pot will continue to present a problem for a society where there are far too few jobs available to those coming into the workplace from our nation's colleges as well as the growing numbers of immigrants entering the labor force. In this and other chapters, I will cover how these generations influence the corporate landscape today. The unemployment rate remains high because the skills acquired by the unemployed fail to match the prerequisite skills needed for specialized careers in high skilled industries. An influx of immigrants, loss of blue and white collar jobs to international growth, infrastructural cost ramifications, production cost, emerging markets, and the fact of older workers remaining in the workplace for extended periods past normal retirement age, will continue to add to the employment dilemma in this country. It will thrust upon companies the need to harness productivity equation of each of these generations and particularly succeed in the brain drain of the Baby Boomers who will, like it or not, leave the workplace in significant numbers over the next 5 years.

Statistics show that today, approximately two percent of those who are first time entries into the workforce will terminate during their first year of employment. Many of these new entries separate from their employer because they are unable to multi task, or they misread the culture and environment during the interview process. Others leave because of the leadership style, or lack thereof, of those in leadership positions. The average turnover rate for all industries is about 24 percent per year. It is higher in the "retail" industry (approx. 40 percent) and slightly lower in others like Transportation (approx. 17 percent) and Manufacturing (approx. 13 percent). No matter the percentage, these turnover figures are a significant cost to any business.

Furthermore, these new entries are, for the first time in history, having to share the workplace with four other generations namely the **_Traditionalist,_** which make up approximately 75 million people, born in the years of 1922 through1945 and many or still gainfully employed. These were the product of the great depression, the G.I Bill, World War II and the cold war. They were loyal to their clients and customers almost to a fault. These were the significant events that were the cornerstone of that generation:

    1937 – Hindenburg tragedy
    1937 – Disney's first animated features (Snow White)
    1941 – Hitler invades Russia, Pearl Harbor, World War II
    1945 – War ends in Europe and Japan
    1947 – Jackie Robinson joined major league baseball
    1950 – Korean War begins

Many in the **Traditional Generation** who are not employed today in major industries across the country are taking entry level positions in the service industry. These are historically positions held by young pre-college teens that are becoming less dependable, absence prone and without passion for what they consider menial labor and a drain on their personal time.

The second group is the **_Baby Boomers_** representing approximately 80 million people many of which entered the workforce between the years 1946 and 1964 and are the standard bearers and corporate leaders of today. In the United States, approximately 80 million babies were born during the Baby Boom. Much of this cohort of nineteen years (1946-1964) grew up with Water Gate, Woodstock, economic prosperity, the Vietnam War, John F. Kennedy as president and the human rights movement.

In 2006, the oldest Baby Boomers were turning 60 years old, including the first two Baby Boomer presidents, Presidents William J. Clinton and George W. Bush, both born in the first year of the Baby Boom, 1946. The dramatic increase in births during the Baby Boom helped to lead to exponential rises in the demand for consumer products, suburban homes, automobiles, roads, and services. Demographer P.K. Whelpton forecast this demand, as quoted in the August 9, 1948 edition of Newsweek. The environment during that time:

Key events of the period:

    1954 - First Transistor Radio
    1960 – Birth control pills introduced
    1962 – John Glen circled the earth
    1963 – Martin Luther King Jr. lead march on Washington
    1963 – President Kennedy assassinated
    1965 – U.S. sent troops to Vietnam
    1966 – Cultural Revolution in China
    1967 – World's first heart transplant
    1969 – U.S. moon landing/Woodstock
    1970 – Women's liberation demonstrations

Next was the **_Generation X'ers_** who makes up approximately 46 million, and represents those born between the years 1965 and 1981. Generation X can technically be defined as the generation following the Baby Boomers. X'ers were born between 1965 and 1980, 1961 and 1981, 1964 and 1979, 1963 and 1979, 1965 and 1975 or since the mid-1960s, depending on the source. So for the sake of this work, we will say that Generation X was born between 1965 and 1980, now ranging in age from 17-32 and usually judged by characteristics assigned to them by the media.

Generation X'ers were brought up on television, Atari 2600s and personal computers. They are the generation that was raised in the 1970s and 1980s, and saw this country undergo a selfish phase that they do not want to repeat. The majority of the generation is experiencing financial difficulties because of the economic down-turn more so that other generations. They took a lot of risk with little reward. By some measures Generation X came out of the latest recession more bruised and battered than other age groups according to some sources. Many were products of divorced parents and suffered the scares as a result. They experienced the scourge of AIDS and crack cocaine more than other generations.

Gen X'ers, those who are about 33 to 45 years old today, saw the biggest drop in net worth from 2005-2010; are struggling with their careers while saddled with college debt; and they're looking nervously in the rear-view mirror at the younger and much more aggressive Generation Y crowd. Key events during that time:

- 1973 – Global energy crisis
- 1976 – Tandy and Apple markets PCs
- 1978 – Mass suicide in Jonestown
- 1979 – Three Mile Island incident
- 1979 – Massive corporate layoffs
- 1980 – John Lennon killed
- 1981 – AIDS identified
- 1986 – Chernobyl disaster

- 1987 – Stock Market plummets
- 1989 – Exxon Valdez oil spill
- 1989 – Berlin Wall falls
- 1989 – Tiananmen Square uprising

Following the X'ers are the **_Millennials_** or Generation Y'ers, who were born between the years 1982 and 2000 and their numbers are close to 80 million. Now I will have to stay on this group for a while because of all the generations, they are the most talented as well as most confusing. In my earlier book, I called these folks the **_Boomeranger_** generation because, like the boomerang, they leave home, try their wings in many work environments. If the new experiences don't suit their need for adventure, they soon return home and usually don't want to leave. It's not uncommon to see these individuals staying home well into their late twenties and early thirties. Generation Y grew up with technology and rely on it to perform their jobs better. Armed with iPhones, Laptops, I-pads and other gadgets, Generation Y is plugged-in 24 hours a day, 7 days a week. This generation prefers to communicate through e-mail and text messaging rather than face-to-face contact and prefers webinars and online technology to traditional lecture-based presentations. This generation has an unending dependency on their parents from sun up to sundown requiring as many as 2-6 hours of reassurance and validation via telephone each day.

"In contrast to previous generations, Millennials are using technology to demand and receive a nearly endless stream of parental affirmations," said behavioral psychologist George Wright, the study's lead author. "Like helpless infants, members of this demographic group instinctively seek out the security of their parents the moment they encounter even the slightest hint of un-happiness, and in most cases cannot fall asleep without the soothing sound of their mother or father's voice flowing directly into their ears." They have the need to ask their parents for advice on every life turn.

- Wright confirmed that members of this age group all appeared to possess a deep-rooted belief that they were unique and special, which innately drove them to demand their parents' full attention at all times, even from thousands of miles away. As a result, millennials reportedly forced their mothers and fathers to receive dozens of calls per day, both at home and at work, and listen patiently as they explained every aspect of their lives, seemingly under the impression that each minute detail of their existence was worthy of exposition and acknowledgment.

Key events during the time period:

- 1990 – Nelson Mandela released
- 1993 – Apartheid ends
- 1995 – Bombing of Federal Bldg. in Oklahoma City
- 1997 – Princess Diana dies
- 1999 – Columbine High School shooting
- 2001 – World Trade Center attacks (911)
- 2002 – Enron, WorldCom and corporate scandals
- 2003 – War begins in Iraq
- 2004 – Tsunami in Asian Ocean
- 2005 – Hurricane Katrina

Generation X, were quite the opposite and spent as few hours talking to the parents as possible. Parents often complained about how little this generation kept in contact. In fact usually when they did call, it was because they had a specific need.

This is much more of a problem than once realized. The traditionalist think a mouse is a rodent; a tweet is a sound that a bird makes and a reboot is having you old pair of boots resoled at the cobblers. It's hard trying to get a generation of Boomers who grew up with their major technology being the typewriter, having to work with and sometime manager the Millennials who value social media like twitter, Facebook and LinkedIn. There are significantly different motivators driving each of the generations resulting in gaps in understanding of what really drives each of them to their ultimate peak performance.

According to the Lancaster report, companies are finding that culture and productivity are being negatively affected by poorly handled generational issues. It cites lack of communication; the tension between, "that's the way we've always done it" and "let's change it because we can"; differences in generational values on issues as diverse as work ethic and dress codes; workforce shifts; and the problem of obtaining and retaining multi-generational talent. I contend that the business who quickly address this growing concern, will ultimately win the intellectual capital (people) war before the Boomers are history.

Let me set the record straight as it relates to available jobs in this country. ***There is not a shortage of jobs***…there is a shortage of job skills. There are many jobs open and have been for a long period of time but there is a skills gap that further promotes the crisis. In a highly technical world, many are seeking the softer none technical skills where the opportunities are few. In careers such as engineering, computer science, science, research, finance, payroll and banking, product design, devices, and quality control, many of these positions are open in excess of 12 months because of skill shortages. You must, if you have the skills, go where the jobs are. You must go to the larger cities like Los Angeles, Chicago, New York and San Francisco which are increasingly finding it hard to attract these talents because of the substantial increase in cost of living as well as quality of life. Many of these young talented resources are choosing smaller more innovative employers where they can make more of an immediate impact and if having made the right selection, can quickly elevate their financial status.

Some companies, having accumulated an array of talent over the years, will face the challenge of retention because of the lack of opportunities to promote at the rate higher enough to sustain their continued dedication and interest. Many of these young and aggressive talents are simply waiting for the economy to improve to make their move to the highest bidder. The old traditional retention tools like stock options and bonuses alone will not retain these new entries. They are more impressed with flexible work schedules, international assignments (expatriate), and leading key company initiatives (project management). They know and have the insight that with these key core skills will come the superior compensation packages as well as stretch job assignments and increased opportunity.

They, unlike the Boomers, are not dedicated to one company but will follow the opportunity as well as the culture and environment of the innovative companies. They are not as concerned about traditional dress, traditional work schedules and the more challenging the assignment the better for them. They are brash, confident and eager to take the lead and show how good they are. They are different. Where most of us can only handle one or two tasks at a time, these new cyber space tech-na-crats can study, listen to MP3s and ride a stationary bike. They are indeed multi task-ers and are quick to declare boredom unless they are continually challenged.

According to Massachusetts-based consultant Tammy Erickson and her new studies of the generations, the next generation to be considered is called, Re-Generation or Re-Gens. This new generation of contributors were born during the mid nineteen-nineties and seems to be trending toward living within their limits instead of depending on credit. According to her research, they are environmental conscious, less dependent on technology, concerned about energy shortage, water shortages and more of a higher sense of responsibility to be more egalitarian and thoughtful about our natural resources. She goes on to say," they are less likely to incur debt, they will defer gratification and less likely to have a need for ownership. The will be more of a save- and –buy generation unlike those before it.

Based on what seems to be this generation's direction, it will be much more entrepreneurial than the prior generations. They will be less mobile by choice, more likely to stay home longer not for security but because of comfort, and finally, not focused on working for the major employers as prior generations. This will be a slow transition to this generation because they are mostly late teens and early twenties. They will be even smarter and more exposed than the Millennials. They will play more of a role in the political and international arena because the world will continue to decrease in virtual size as it globalizes. As we could observe from the economic crisis, if the European sector catches a cold, the United States is exposed to the flu.

CHAPTER II
READING THE ENVIRONMENT

> *"What matters isn't being applauded when you arrive – for that is common - but being missed when you leave".*
>
> —*Baltasar Gracian*

For those of you preparing to graduate from college or changing jobs where new environments are involved, this book should be in your library or better still in your back pack. Individuals coming into new work environments immediately have to deal with new clients, colleagues, work streams and the expectation that they will hit the ground running in a very short period of time. Their first 90 days are spent justifying whether they had made the correct decision in joining the organization while the organization does the same through probation period.

The elements of adaptation related to company culture, location layout, key clients and customers, must be understood in order to make a seamless transition to a new culture. In addition to these conditions, new entrants to the workforce will continually face fewer opportunities; stagnant salary actions; stretch assignments because of low staffing levels; cost constraints; low or no bonuses and longer work hours.

There are environments that are in need of people who are chameleons. A chameleon is a small reptile that changes color to adapt to its surroundings and environment. The color change is a protective mechanism for survival in the wild. In a sense, we all have to adapt the characteristics of this small reptile as we navigate the tricky, murky and sometime confusing waters of the corporate work environment. Many individuals jump into these waters only to find that they are not buoyant enough to sustain themselves in deep and difficult situations. Some didn't realize that they were getting in over their heads and once too far from shore or their competency level was not adequate, could not adjust readily resulting in dissatisfaction, unhappiness and eventually drown or suffer irreversible paralysis.

It's not practical to think that you can learn to swim after you have been thrown overboard. The time to really learn is prior to getting into the water. If you know that you can't swim, at least be smart enough to put on a life jacket. The life gear that I am referring to is building your competency tool kit. These competencies include but are not limited to: 1) project management skills 2) effective presentation skills 3) multi-lingual skills 4) technical capability 5) computer savvy 6) effective in social media and 7) understanding accounting and balance sheets. In addition to these traits, one must be confident, mobile, and aggressive, with strong corroborative skills and a magnetic personality. A lot to ask, you may add, but asking they will.

What I am sharing in this short resource manual is helping individuals to properly strap on their life jacket. Being able to swim gives you options when you are in the water. You can freestyle, swim on your back, use the breath stroke, dog paddle, or simply tread water. In corporate America, developing your competencies in finance, information systems, project management and negotiating skills support your primary competency and give you options to move through the sometimes difficult currents existing in the rough and competitive waters of the corporate environment.

The road to success starts in the early years of elementary and high school when your values are solidified and your study and behavioral habits becomes your brand. Your brand has an external flair. It's what others think of you that promotes or tarnish your brand and not as much your thoughts of yourself. Your behavior is more than half the battle. It not only affects the success equation but also affects how others interact with your brand. You start early in developing your brand through learning and behaving in a socially acceptable manner. A good ***attitude*** (our behavior and, demeanor)*,* can leads to increased ***aptitude*** (the ability to grasp and learn) which intern can lead to a higher ***altitude*** (how high we can climb).

Early in the college years, it is imperative that top performers identify corporations that are willing to work with the school either through arranged coop assignments or through summer intern relationships. These opportunities should begin as soon as the freshman year is completed. I suggest not attempting these internship until the sophomore year of college because the freshman year should be reserved for gaining your sea legs, learning the ropes, developing good study habits and establishing consistency in your presence in this new and challenging environment. It is also important that there is a diversity of assignments within a company or with different companies, to facilitate holistic learning in distinct and different corporate cultures.

Many companies have differences in expectations of work time, organizational structures, leadership attributes, and management styles that are not immediately understood. A lack of ability to quickly assimilate to a new culture could be a career game-changer or, in corporate terminology, a derailer to their long-term career aspirations. Understanding the social, technical, and political climates in an organization is critical to navigating the corporate climate. Many of these awareness skills are developed early and while still on campus. Internships and cooperative assignments are critical in developing these awareness skills. We will discuss these in more detail later in the manual.

Many students, because of lack of direction, do not utilize the valuable resources available on campus such as student outplacement centers, coaches or counselors, co-ops, summer internships and other available support systems that are key tools in the preparation stages. Schools could benefit tremendously from a strategy which includes more focus on diversity management. Now what do you mean by diversity management you might ask? Well, no matter the diversity of the campus, once in the work world, it's not just seeing and communicating with people of difference, it's working in teams and maximizing the potential of diverse cultures. It's truly seeking to understand the cultural specific drivers and embracing the dynamics of this social melting pot.

It's not easy having the lion lay down with the lamb if you understand the metaphor. Many young people are placed into diverse environments for the first time of any significance without coping skills or without valuing differences that exist between cultures. Many companies are ill prepared to train in the area of diversity further amplifying the situation. Working with groups that one has not been exposed to can be both an opportunity and stressful without proper training and satisfaction of business and personal expectations being met. Now we set the stage for the true environment post college assimilation.

Companies sometime choose to define diversity in the narrowest sense. Diversity was presented as something that primarily was designed for women and other minority cultures with the exception of white males. It also carries the connotation of being "less than" or "given special treatment". What a tremendous mistake that is being made if that's how diversity is defined holistically. Diversity is an ingredient found in all of us no matter our race, sex, color or national origin. Size, weight, race, culture, talent, ability are all facets of diversity. Any exclusion is an attack on true and real diversity. The new definition of diversity is rooted in the words "inclusion" as well as focusing on our similarities verses our differences. Differences are not to be taken for granted and I am not suggesting that we exclude it. What I do mean is that we must value and respect our differences while celebrating those things that are consistent within us all no matter our backgrounds and or cultures.

In addition to these hurdles, new entries are dealing with multi cultures and multi generational issues. Baby Boomers, in growing numbers, are extending their careers not by choice but because their 401k retirement funds are not as robust as originally planned and are shrinking as the economy retracts. As a result, older managers are required to manage and lead a much younger work teams having different goals, life styles, and work ethics. With there being fewer of the traditional qualified retirement plans available because of corporate cost pressures, many are depending on 401K plans which, in many cases, have a risk factor driven by the heavy dependency on stock portion of the plan. That premise coupled with the growing concern related to the longevity threat to stability of social security, has caused a lengthening of careers on the part of boomers. That fact will automatically bring them into growing conflicts with the new cultural change pressures and faster moving and more demanding environments.

Companies are asking these aging gladiators to train, motivate and energize these younger generations who are technically savvy, less loyal and more strategic that they could ever imagine. This dilemma is being played out through both the domestic and international sectors and the company that is successful in solving this generational equation will be on the leading edge of successful group dynamics. A combination of the extensive experience and dedication of the boomers and the technical and strategic sophistication of the X's and Y's makes for a very productive, challenging and exceedingly difficult work place.

This is one of the most challenging initiatives facing management today. Making decisions on how to manage people of different cultures, different levels of competencies as well as different generations, presents a daunting business scenario. In this current economy of more competition, fewer jobs, outsourcing driven by cost pressures and less make(Promotion from within) and more buy (hiring externally), management must stay focused on leadership style and command if they are to stay ahead of the game.

These older workers who are also being asked to team with and in many cases work for these new entries who are hungry, ambitious and impatient grads seeking leadership opportunities right now and that's not soon enough. These young and hungry tigers again are bringing an attitude of impatience, work smarter not harder philosophy and less time spent physically on the job. They are asking for and taking more personal time of, working flex schedules, accepting expatriate assignments abroad, and taking on complex tasks that are outside their comfort levels. These are in direct contrast to the boomers who are use to staying on jobs longer, remaining with one employer for long periods of time and afraid of flex time for fear of the "out of site out of mind" perception. These older workers are less likely to accept, if offered, international assignments; fearful of risk-taking; and reluctant to share with the younger entries for fear of losing job security.

Many dual degree graduates from the top business and law schools are entering the workplace demanding six figure salaries and getting it simply because of the competition for their skills and the demand for their talents. Their accelerated salaries come in immediate conflict with older workers that have earned their salaries through longevity and experience. These newer workers are the future leaders and companies are forced to attract them with higher salaries and benefits. These actions on the part of companies are primarily for the purpose of remaining competitive and retaining the higher caliber talent in a very tight and more specialized talent pool. The downside to the dilemma is that older workers are looking to external organizations like the Equal Employment Opportunity Commission as well as the Office of Federal Compliance (OFCCP) and state labor boards, to act on their behalf in age discrimination litigation. More and more minority, women, aged and military resources are forcing the hand of companies to recognize their contributions to the workplace. This is while continuing to work for the company creating tension within the ranks.

As a result of these actions, older workers are feeling handcuffed and less marketable, along with their deteriorating desire to dance to the fast pace music of the new more strategic and ambiguous work environment. Many companies fall into the trap of releasing older workers with higher salaries because they can get an even greater skill set from younger workers at lower salary and benefit levels. The legal troubles starts as a result of companies releasing these older workers prior to their qualifying for retirement which often also results in expensive litigation. These early retirements represents a loss of skills and competencies, many of which are not properly documented and resides in the minds of these older resources.

Jack Welch, the retired CEO and Chairman of the General Electric Corporation, believed that in order to maintain a competitive edge and retain you key talent base, there has to be a "weeding" of the workforce each year. Jack had, what we in the HR community called, the 10-40-40-10 retention plan. Each year there should be the top ten percent of the workforce that moves out to other positions with greater responsibility. A new ten percent moves up from the upper forty percent to replace those leaving. Ten percent from the lower forty percent move up to take their places. Another ten percent of the bottom forty moves to the lower ten percent because they could not maintain their skill edge and the bottom ten percent are exited from the company because of their inability to keep up with a changing and more demanding environment.

In this system, the company is constantly replenishing its talent pool and in corporate jargon, "constantly reinventing itself". It may sound a little harsh but it works. What a system like that does is require a person to, each year, continue to raise their level of performance in order to maintain their status with the organization. In other words, those who are the valued and cherished resource, are able to successfully apply for their jobs on an annual basis and retain it because they are able to keep their skills relevant.

Older workers tend to be more the victim of the purging because of unwillingness to upgrade their skill tool kit on an ongoing basis. They tend to be more satisfied with the status quo and just doing a good job when the new environment requires those progressing in the organization to seek higher and higher ground. Their unwillingness to do so has created what corporations call "Blockers". Blockers are those who have reached the final **altitude** in their careers and tend to be satisfied where they are. Companies need many of these positions for developing future leaders so are forced to move these aged warriors to other less impactful positions creating dissatisfaction and increased litigation based on perceived age discrimination.

Baby Boomers, who still hold a significant portion of leadership roles in major companies, will have to face the growing pressure of keeping current on job skills and management styles if they are to lead through a generation of those using social media like Twitter, LinkedIn, Skype and Facebook. These cyber geniuses, who have broken the old adage of complete communications and are satisfied with short sound bites and tweets, are taking their rightful place as successors to a powerful generation of Boomers that blazed a wide and well developed trail….. that is until now.

As we move into the new millennium, boomers will have to raise their game and learn to work with and manage this new and powerful resource base that is not as dedicated to one company. They value personal time more than boomers have and aren't afraid to challenge the status quo. These new talented resources are more accustomed to communicating via the web site and these other new social mediums rather than face to face which has been the preferred mode of communicating by prior generations.

This new workforce is brash, confident, strategic, refined and impatient. These "young Guns" tend to work well in teams of quick learners, risk takers and outspoken critics. Many of these traits are not consistent with the transmission that has driven the Boomers engines for the last couple of decade. The boomers were dedicated, respectful, and less mobile. They would stay with one company for twenty to thirty years because of that dedication. The new workforce goes with the highest bidder. Boomers in many cases would stay put instead of taking opportunities in other companies and locations simply because of loyalty. Many never felt the need to take international assignments which are significant to growing and managing a talented but impatient culture of young, diverse employees.

What I will share with you thus far are some hopefully creative ideas on how to access the correct position in the boat to help navigate you to a successful career in Corporate America. There is no magic formula that will guarantee your name being on a plaque on the business wall after you are done. What I can do is share experiences, suggestions, resources and directions from many who have traveled these difficult but rewarding roads before you. Acquiring the knowledge from the generation before you is a recommended activity. A combination of a little of the old school experience and knowledge with new concepts and creativity from the new school, makes for a rich and rewarding outcome. Companies that solve the problem of retaining the Boomers long enough to experience the brain drain will most likely run ahead of the pack and maintain their human intellectual properties.

This short manual is written in the spirit of assisting those who lack the integrative skills needed to chart the course to success in the highly volatile and globally competitive world of corporate America. I have spent many hours talking to individuals who have successfully navigated these waters as well as those who are still on deck trying to find their water wings as they chart their own individual courses. These pages also cover some who became casualties when their skills did not match the culture and needs of a particular business. I sometimes had to strap on my scuba gear to find those who were caught in the perfect storm and became casualties of the system and eventually sunk to the bottom of the corporate ocean.

There are many rungs on the ladder to success and you must pick the rung that works best for your reaching the top. Each ladder has different heights, different trajectory. No one's ladder is the same. Each of us is unique in our methods, mind set, background and capability. That's what gives the melting pot spice and the meal that much more satisfying as we navigate these challenges in the world of corporate opportunities. Where companies, years ago, spend countless hours development career ladders and career development processes, these tools became increasingly expensive and were eliminated driving individuals to take charge of their own career development. Without proper coaching and advice many individuals made ill-fated decisions causing a set back to their career.

CHAPTER III
THE SUCCESSFUL BEGINNING

"People who know how to employ themselves, always find leisure moments, while those who do nothing are forever in a hurry".

—*Jeanne Marie Roland*

Many young college graduates leave college for the work world with only limited knowledge of what awaits them as they venture into a highly competitive and unforgiving world of uncertainty. When young people move from high school to college, the changes that are encountered are drastic. Those who are able to maintain their study habits and minimize the distractions are starting to develop the kind of independent and holistic thinking that will lead them to a satisfying end. Going off to college for the first time is when you experience, sometimes for the first time, that of not having someone tell you to get out of bed, get dressed, or to study for an exam. In college, you have to make those decisions on your own. You have finally left the nest. Your wings are well defined and you are now starting to develop your own flight path and chart your own course leading toward finally mastering your own fate.

From this point forward; who you associate with; how you act and what you decide to involve yourself in, starts the maturation of your brand. Branding will be your signature for the rest of your working life. There will be times when your brand will need calibrating but changing your brand can sometime be impossible or difficult at the least. Your brand becomes your signature, your Tattoo. I will explore in more detail the whole Branding process as its effect on careers as we move further into the chapter.

As mentioned earlier, one true and proven way of giving a candidate a decent shot at a position with a company is through arranged internship or cooperatives. With these programs, companies will get the opportunity to observe your abilities, your competencies and your project management skills while you work on key initiatives and strategic milestones having short cycle times. These project management skills are particularly critical to your successful entry into most corporate structures. How you handle key initiative from inception to closure will be the trademark of your upward mobility index.

Companies seeking the competitive edge are leaning toward those individuals who have the technical as well as interpersonal and relationship skills in their area of expertise. These companies are looking for those having the ability to quickly grasp the environment, understand and navigate the politics, as well as lead teams of diverse resources to a planned project end. Also, more and more companies are seeking individuals who are multilingual and who are flexible in thought, reasonably mobile with strong teaming skills and willing to take risk to further the advancement of their clients as well as the company at large. What a tall order but many of the leading edge companies are finding what they are looking for and are willing to pay the price to get them.

New MBA graduates in particular are most often successfully at navigating these turbulent waters primarily because of the rigorous curriculum required in good business schools as well as acquiring key internships over a two to three year period while finishing their degrees. They tend to value the need to maintain their competency edge through seeking continued education and development opportunities. Staying abreast of current market trends, reading the business magazines and networking plays a key role in separating those who hold a job and those who enhance their careers. The success equation does not stop upon graduation. In fact, it is just beginning to blossom and your competitive juices must flow to keep pace in a more sophisticated and strategic corporate culture.

Each of us has things of significance that someone we truly respect has shared with us. I have one such experience from my past. I remember a cliché that one of my mentors Steve Dolny shared with me. That cliché that I referenced was called the Pike Syndrome. A pike is a large aggressive fish that feed off of other species. He would say," if you take a Pike and place it into a large tank and put smaller fish in with it, within minutes, the Pike would consume all of the smaller fish. But if you take that same situation and place the small fish in a smaller tank within the larger tank and place the Pike in the larger tank, the Pike would bump against the glass of the smaller tank continuously trying to get to the smaller fish. After a while it would float to the bottom, exhausted from trying unsuccessfully to get to get a meal. Once the pike has exhausted itself, you could then release the smaller fish from the smaller tank within the larger tank. The Pike would then sink to the bottom of the tank and die of starvation because it is afraid to test its assumption. It still assumes that it cannot get to the smaller fish". Unfortunately Steve passed away a few years ago but his teachings live on in me and many others whose lives were touched by this visionary.

I include this metaphor in many of my works because it's so applicable to human development on many levels. That example was truly an eye opener for me because we all make assumptions and because of fear of inadequacy or failure, we are afraid to test our assumption and venture out in unchartered waters. We assume that we cannot survive in certain situations or certain industries. We are paralyzed by fear of failure.

Only those comfortable in their own skin, confident, secure in their competencies can successfully negotiate these difficult corporate waters.

Life and a career is somewhat like that pike. Those who are afraid to take risk, or try something new and different, or who are afraid to express their opinions, are doomed to the "Pike syndrome". Those who test their assumptions will usually get rewarded for stepping out on faith, taking risk and reaping their just reward. Many companies like GE, IBM or Microsoft get out ahead of the pack through investing in sophisticated training programs that allow the company to assess the newly identified talent through multi assignments over a given period. I was a product of the General Electric program and I can tell you that it was one of the most rewarding experiences of my working career.

First of all, to be selected into this program was an accomplishment within itself. During my tenure with the General Electric Company, which lasted twenty five years, there were but 50 positions each in Finance, Human Resources, Marketing and Information Technology that are available yearly in this elite process and the competition for these few positions were fierce and down-right nerve racking. Knowing someone within the company was a big help but you had to interview well and convince the leaders of the program that you were worthy of the opportunity to become a part of what soon became a fraternity and sorority of talented young minds who would not only excel in their professions but would develop a bond that has stood throughout our careers.

Many of the individuals who, like myself, were given this gift of experience, by General Electric, are still networking with each other today even though we are scattered in companies across the globe. We share ideas, networks, opportunities and a personal bond that is unbreakable. Many young people take off their caps and gowns from rigorous mental exercises and competitive forays with their classmate at the many college and universities across the country, to jump on the corporate train without being properly prepared for the journey. This apply particular to many who come from smaller universities and those that are predominately minority cultures. Preparatory courses that can be found on the majority of the larger universities may or may not be available at smaller educational entities.

Many colleges and universities have resources whose primary responsibility is working with industries to establish both summer internships and cooperative programs to aid the students in networking their skills and overall packaging. Schools that are not particularly resource rich will not have the human of financial capital are forced to leave those preparatory activities strictly to the individual. Those individuals are now left in the blocks, (an old track & field term meaning starting the race very slowly and behind the others). Other more fortunate students have agents working on their behalf and in many cases will achieve considerable success while the less prepared individuals are sometimes led deeper into despair from the lack of intervention.

Let's be clear, I am not indicating that these students are any less qualified than those coming from major colleges. Most often, they are not as prepared based on the lack of available prep courses and their inability to compete with the more prepared blue chip college resources for dwindling cooperative and internship opportunities. According to a survey published recently by Adecco, a global human resources firm, 66 percent of hiring managers believe that recent graduates are prepared for the challenges of the current workplace. Another 58 percent of the hiring managers feel that it's fruitless to hire the current crop of graduates because of that premises. Additional surveys tend to follow that or similar logic. Many other surveys conducted by the National Association of Colleges conclude that employers will only hire 2.1 to 2.5 percent more of the class of 2013 as compared to 2012. That number according to the survey is 10 percent lower than estimated.

Most large corporations are seeking the best and the brightest which they view, more often than not, as resourced coming from major universities such as Harvard, Yale, MIT, Brown, Duke, Michigan, Ohio State, Columbia, Purdue, Penn State and other blue chip colleges and universities. Many of the very talented rich smaller schools often are not on the list for consideration and have a more difficult time placing their top students. This is a greater problem for company seeking to diversify its workforce because these major universities are not rich with the diversity talent that tends to exist in smaller schools. Many good students attend smaller universities and colleges not because of their inability to qualify at the larger schools but because of availability of necessary financial resources.

CHAPTER IV
THE INTERVIEW PROCESS

"Nothing contributes so much to tranquilize the mind as a study purpose – a point of which the soul may fix its intellectual eye".

—Mary Shelley

In this chapter we will explore these success areas/characteristics. Each of these characteristics will surely have an impact on the successful or failed entry into the workplace. In more cases than not, during the interview process, it is not always the most qualifies individual who eventually gets the job. Most successes comes from individuals that have committed themselves to the process through proper preparation of their resume, getting an inside track either through a current employee referral, through a major placement firm or through earlier suggestions of internships or cooperatives. The individual having the ability to sell based on personality, presence, competencies, experience and their extracurricular depth and breadth, most often makes it through the initial waves and undercurrents of the introductory process. Now let's visit some of these key success tools.

The Resume

First let's consider the presentation of the resume. As a human resources leader, I review a considerable number of resumes that are poorly written, structurally inadequate, run on and run off sentences, poor spelling (spell check will not always pick up poor sentence structure or misplaced words.), flawed format and often omitted key pieces of information. Many of these resumes have gaps in the experience data without explanation; improper use of words and often the content have no relevance to the job in question. Additionally many use the resume to highlight their responsibilities on past job assignments but fail to include the accomplishments against those responsibilities. Companies are most interested in how the company of record had benefited from you presence verses simply knowing what your job responsibilities were. For those students coming right out of college, you should show your versatility by including on campus jobs and courses that are particular relevant to the job at hand. The resume should be written to display your competencies directly or indirectly addressing the core requirements of the position at hand. Needless to say, every element of the resume should be truthful and explainable. Your resume is part of your personal brand (there is that word again) and an introduction to parts of your experience base. Think of the resume as your introducing yourself for the first time and what impression is left after you depart. The key to any introduction is not as much what's said while you are there but what is said after you leave.

The resume is a precursor to the face to face interview and determines whether there will be a next step in the interview process. Many resumes are tossed simply because they can not stand the acid test as stated above. Take the time to invest in having your resume professional done if you are not confident that you will put out a quality product. Remember that first impression is lasting. Proper structure, even the font of the computer generated copy, has an effect on the overall appearance and effectiveness of the final product. If you choose to do it yourself seek proper formatting and contend help from the internet or from reliable professional resources. Stay away from loud and colorful paper which can be distracting from the content.

Have another set of eyes, versed in resume' writing, take a final look before submitting for an identified opportunity. Always gear your resume to the stated needs of the position in question. One should not assume that the person reviewing the resume will pick out the relevant information so it's the resume' owner's responsibility to highlight prerequisite skills. It wouldn't hurt to have several people look at your resume before submitting. Remember, sometimes several fresh sets of critical eyes can catch weaknesses that you may have missed. You are generally too familiar with the content to catch all of the structural pot holes in the document.

Remember, the resume is your ticket to the big dance. It opens the door for further exploration of your abilities. Many candidates never get past the resume submittal stage because of flaws in the document. Another fatal mistake made on many resumes is placing data strictly to impress the interviewer. Everything on the resume should be related to an actual experience on a particular job or work task. You should be intimate with all facets of the information on the resume. Make sure that you are able to answer any questions related to information included on the document.

No matter how much you feel that you know yourself, take the time prior to the interview to study the resume and ask yourself the questions that you feel may be asked by the interviewer. One final note; it always help to arrange the experience and work history in descending order with your current experience first insuring that the time frames between each position leaves no gaps. Your resume is a part of your brand. It's the paper version of a portion of your life's work. The quality and appearance of the document, its integrity and impact on the viewer may be the window to a bright future or a dismal existence. Once your resume has passed the scrutiny of the consultants or human resources person, the next initiative is usually the phone interview.

Many companies are relying on social media to identify potential resources. Though they still utilize recruiting firms to surface candidates, there are increasing trends toward social media. This trend should not be taken lightly. Many individuals use mediums like Facebook, Tweeter and LinkedIn as ways to socialize and keep in touch with friends a family. While on these site, many place information that's inappropriate from a business perspective. Many recruiters and companies use these new high tech mediums as part of their background check process and particularly as a way to locate hard to find talent. It is recommended that you not place information on your site that you wouldn't want a perspective employer to see. Inappropriate pictures, statements, invites can be a recipe for a lost opportunity.

Periodically edit your site and delete those contacts that will not play by your rules. Remember what you display on your site becomes part of your individual brand and can tarnish the product to a point where employers will keep their distance. Many of these social media are what companies are, in increasing numbers, turning to for recruiting. Many of these social tools allow companies to automatically post their opportunities, seek talented resources from their competitors and track talent to a level never seen before.

The Phone Screen

Before I get started on the phone screen, please, please make your schedule is flexible enough to accept the call from the managing resource for the position. Many candidates miss prime opportunities base on availability or failure to follow up on important calls from professional staffing organizations. You are not the only character in this play. There are others waiting in the wings to get your part if you fumble through your lines.

There are two types of phone screens that may be encountered. The first being the one conducted by the recruiting firm tasked with locating candidates for the employer. They tend to be the initial screeners to determine if a candidate is worthy of being presented to the employer. These interviews tend to be very high level and focuses on the required qualifications for the position. This individual will determine the top two or three candidates to present to the employer. Failure to impress these "point" men and women will cause an early derailment of the process. They will explore your interest in the company, the location and type of position. They will ask questions to validate what was found from their parasail of your resume. Did your conversation fit the resume? Do you speak at a level consistent with the level and responsibility of the job at hand? Are you comfortable explaining your current responsibilities?

The second type of phone screen is with the employer, usually someone in staffing. This discussion will focus more on the resume, knowledge about the company in general terms as well as your reason for applying for the position. This interview is primarily to probe a bit into you interest in the position, to ask questions that comes from the initial reading of you resume and to find out how your competencies compare to the basic requirements of the position. Did you take serious the interview to a point of research on the company such as yearly sales, market cap, return on sales, employment levels, markets, customers, competitors, major products, stock historical trends, etc?

Many interviewers are interested in how worldly you are by asking about current events in the news related to government activity, the economy, or even major world events. This allows the interviewer to check the breadth and depth of you maturity, your interest in world matters and your bandwidth of learning. It also is that point where the candidate start injecting proof of his/her research into the company's key measures such as competitors, market data, population, revenue, etc.

The Face to Face Interview Proper Dress

Let's consider reasons why some individuals have a misstep in their face to face initial entry. Many individuals are derailed before they start because of inappropriate appearance/dress, poor planning or poor time management. It's always appropriate to wear professional dress to an interview no matter the culture unless specifically directed toward clearly articulated casual attire by the person setting up the process. For men, a dark or grey suit and appropriate tie with shoes polished is appropriate and recommended. People have been successful with an altogether different venue but this is the preferred and recommended attire. Please no athletic shoe wear unless instructed to do so because of some predetermined activity that has been scheduled as part of the interview process. Stay away from excessive jewelry.

For the women, similar dress applies. A dark blue or grey suit or dress and the appropriate foot wear. Use appropriate judgment on accessories such as jewelry. The simpler you dress to the basic business requirements, the better. Too much jewelry also can be distracting to the overall purpose. You want the focus of the interview to be on what you are saying, your qualifications for the position, and not your outfit. Low cut or short revealing attire is not recommended. Keep the focus on your competencies and ability, not your appearance. The appearance, though important, is secondary to your qualifications. Remember, first impressions are lasting.

Taking notes

During the interview, always carry a pad and pen for note taking. Key discussion points should be captured so that you can review what was covered without having to depend on an imperfect memory. Many of these facts will be needed as you contemplate the company as your place of employment. Always carry a portfolio of your work especially those things that focuses on your qualifications for the position or past projects that give indication of your skills.

It is also imperative that you arrive on time for the interview. There is nothing worse than a poor first impression of not valuing time. That should apply to both the interview as well as the interviewee. Time is money and wasting it is the business equivalent of affecting the bottom line. Once it's gone, we can't get it back. Once there is an opinion of your lack of time management, that impression may be the difference between success and failure where there are equally qualified candidates.

If you are staying at a hotel in the area, make sure that the taxi or limo is schedule to pick you up with plenty of time to spare. Allow for poor direction, traffic patterns and other unforeseen delays. Try to arrive no less than 30 minutes before the interview giving you time to find the correct location of the interview, to settle down and collect your thoughts while establishing your game plan for the event. One key point here is to get plenty rest the night before so that you are fresh and alert.

It is recommended that you research specifics of the company which you are interviewing. It's important that you show your complete dedication to the process and that the opportunity is valued enough to research the nomenclature of the company such as its history, employment size, revenue, market cap, key competitors, global status and percent of the markets that the company participates in, as was mentioned earlier.

I can feel already that you are more comfortable now than you were a few pages ago (a slight smile should go right here). It's important that the interviewee know their most important subject and that subject is self. Many who go through the interview process are stifled by questions about their personal past, their resume, and their past jobs or responsibilities that should be second nature to them. Study your resume before the interview; know date and times of past jobs and experiences. Most interviewers start the interview with your summarizing your past. You have to be comfortable enough with the data to speak openly and freely about specifics of the resume while the interviewer is checking your facts from the document. All of these early actions and activities start to develop that first impression which can propel you either deeper into the interview process or become a derailer and shorten the process.

Early in the process, the 9-1-1 of the interviewee becomes evident as the word starts to get around to others on the interview schedule. Believe it; the word starts to get around about the quality of the earlier interviews. Personality takes many forms such as how easy the candidate is to talk too? How comfortable is the candidate in his/her skin? How well did the candidate answer questions? Were he/she too busy talking that they didn't effectively listen? Were they prepared for the interview with a set of questions of their own? Do they show that they are excited to be given the opportunity and are they wearing a pleasant smile? Are they properly dressed? You may not think that this happens but it does so take that to the bank and deposit it for future withdrawals.

Next come "**presence**" and competency which within themselves are critical to the successful interview. It is a fact that first impression tends to be lasting. Some people can come into a room and all eyes immediately focus on them while others are invisible upon entering. Presence starts your behavior, your ability to verbalize, the appropriate dress and how you engage in the overall conversation. "**Presence**" is something that some have and some don't. Some will get it through experience and some won't. It is a characteristic that makes a huge difference throughout one's career. It tends to take the shape of one who is confident, charismatic and comfortable in his or her skin.

I have heard many leaders describe attributes of some of their managers like this; "He or she has all the technical skills and competencies but lacks political savvy and executive presence". This "**presence**" comes as a result of your daily walk. You can't just have it when you need it? It's with you all the time. It's in your DNA, your brand. How you carry yourself, how you dress, your speech, personality and your competence all are ingredients of your "presence". These make up your personal brand. Are you still with me? An individual who has a large dose of this leadership love potion has the ability to impact the outcome of events and influence change and above all…influence careers.

We are hearing more and more about individuals in the corporate ranks not having "Executive Presence". What does it really mean and how do you know whether you have it or not. Some see it as how a person dresses; how they present themselves, (presentation skills); leadership, and social skills.

Recognizing the elements of Executive Presence:

- **Vision and Focus** – *The ability to establish a direction and communicate it in a clear and concise manner with a focus on short and long term goals. Good leaders don't just stop with communicating these key factors, they test for understanding. If you can envision success…you can get there. Once you can see it, it's then time to plan your strategy in getting there.*

- **Passion** – *Self motivation, drive and energy toward a goal. You have to want it. Passion keeps one on the path to mission accomplishment .Passion drives you to a different level of performance and modifies the vision. Without passion, your engine will lose steam and eventually and suffer paralysis.*

- **Self Confidence** – *An air of optimism and assurance that an individual can do what they commit without fear of failure. A person that is comfortable in their own skin tends to do well here. Self- confidence is not….arrogance. It's a higher order and takes the form of leading from the front verses boasting about your abilities. A leader in the military is not defined by the stripes on his or her sleeve but instead by their ability to get others to follow no matter the number of stripes.*

- **Risk Taker** – *The ability to step out on faith and engage business issues without fear of reprisal. Stepping out of your normal comfort zone. Having the courage to step away from the crowd to play devil's advocate if it challenges the team to think differently. These individuals are not afraid to take the road less traveled when they* come to the fork. They thrive on new challenges and adventure and are always seeking higher ground.

- **Candor** – Speaking one's mind in a candid and professional way understanding how to incorporate the political aspects of a challenge. Not having fear of asking the tough question in key discussions with people of power.

- **Poise** - Having a sophistication about one's self that reeks of self-confidence; Calm under pressure; Not allowing others to take you out of the game; Thinking before you act.

- **Approachability** – Having a personality, attitude, personal style that would allow others to seek your guidance. Making yourself availability to those seeking your presence. Willing to give of your experience with others in need.

- **Strong Values** – Those foundational substantive values; being true to your word; honesty; truthful; thoughtful; sincerity; trustworthy; etc. The substance and backdrop of your brand.

- **Presence** – Your actions makes those around you better performers. Have the ability to both speak with authority and listen with respect. Others know when you enter the room and happy that you are there. They acknowledge your presence and seek your advice.

- **Appearance** – Dress in a way that is appropriate to the environment and professional culture that you are a part of. Look the professional part. First impressions are lasting. Once opinions are constructed, they are hard to change.

- **Social Style** – Act, in a social setting, in a way that is respectful and indicative of your rank and values. Not willing to tarnish the individuals or company's brand with your behavior.

- ***High level communications and influencing skills*** - The ability to verbally and visually present complex issues to senior executives in a concise and informative way. To withstand and defend executive questioning on issues while not appearing defensive. Be open to criticism and questioning but respond with confidence and courage.

> *"If you want to create impressions that make false messages appear sincere, or project qualities that aren't there, you are almost sure to fail"*
>
> —Paul Aldo, Ph.D.

Interviewers also look for individuals who not only can do the job at hand but also have the career altitude to move higher in the organization. The also look for those individuals who are able to carry extra curricular activities outside their school work or job which gives the interviewer a look at the flexibility of the individual and a clue into his or her ability to multi-task as well as assess the debt and breadth of their capabilities.

There are some things you want to steer away from in the interview:

- **How much does the position pay?** Pay discussions should come much later in the interview process. If the interviewer brings it up, then and only then is it appropriate to enter into dialogue on the subject. Impress upon the interviewer that your primary interest, at this point, is the specifics of the position in question and the competencies needed to succeed in the position. If the company enters into the discussion on pay, it's usually a sign of major interest. In the offer process, there will be plenty of time to negotiate parts of the total compensation and signing package. Entering into pay discussions too early could signal that your focus is financial and not the specifics of the job in question.

- **Being critical of your current management or organization.** If you are so willing to criticize the current system or leader, it may be an indication of what you will do at the new location. Whatever the reason for your leaving the old organization, keep your reason focused on the new opportunity, growth possibilities and the future. Reasons such as improved opportunity, company's culture and direction are more plausible explanations. Guide the discussion toward the positive of your past work experience and less on those things that were not as pleasing. Looking forward keeps you from bumping into something. Looking back takes your focus off the objective.

- **Giving the impression that you are just shopping around.** Never say that you are currently happy in your present position but decided to interview just for the experience. Why waste your time or that of the interviewer because you never know what the future may bring. You may need the contact at a later day. Never burn bridges before you cross them. That kind of attitude gives the impression of arrogance and over confidence and does not play well with most interviewers. If in the course of the interview, it is determined that there is little interest in the position, immediately share your disconnection with the interviewer so as to not waste the time of the others in the interview chain. It is proper to state, "if other opportunities of interest arise that is consistent with my background and competence, please consider me because I am very impressed with the company and its brand". It's a sign of maturity, integrity and respect to the process.

- **Become too familiar or playful with the interviewer.** The interview is a serious ordeal and should be handled with the utmost of respect and professionalism. Though the interviewer may participate in the fun and games, it leaves the impression of a lack of professional behavior and failure to take the process seriously. The interviewer will most often allow you to go and play in someone else's sandbox if you appear to casual. Always approach the interview with a sense of respect and openness but never fall into the trap of feeling too familiar with the interviewer. A pleasant smile and gesture is appropriate without going overboard. The interviewer will set the tone but in the case where the interviewer is acting unprofessional, keep your composure, stick to the script of letting him or her know of your sincere interest and hope that your calmness and direct approach will get the interview back on track.

- **Absolutely do not chew gum during the interview.** It is unprofessional and distracting to the process. It gives the interviewer the impression of your decision making competence and ability to process in an effective manner. Chewing gum will "smack" you right out of contention for the position.

- **Take over the interview by talking too much.** Too much information can frustrate the interviewer and can quickly move you down in the pack of candidates. It is totally appropriate to take notes. It shows a sense of interest and value to the process. Too much talking can give a sense that there are weak listening skills. Many candidates tend to talk because they are nervous and lack self confidence. Answer questions as detailed as possible but in a direct and succinct manner, then wait for the next question. The interviewer may not signal that you are talking excessively but his/her behavior will change to reflect the new climate of "too much" that has just been created. Less is more in this case so pick your spots and don't over communicate.

- **Do not answer questions without thinking.** It is totally acceptable to pause prior to giving an answer. Make completely sure that you have understood the question before giving the answer. There is nothing wrong with asking to have the question repeated. Giving a wrong answer is a sign often of a poor listener. A pause can give you enough time to organize your thoughts and smoothly transition into the answer. If a questioned is asked that you feel you can't answer, admit it and move on instead of giving rambling rhetoric which is even more damaging.

Things you should do during and after the interview.

- Do take notes and come prepared with a copy of your resume and portfolio of any specific and pertinent documents related to the interview. Sometimes the interviewer, in the midst of a busy day, may not have completed the reading of the resume and may not have it at hand. It is important to have the document as a reference if questions do come up that the resume can clarify. Other information that clearly shows your pass experience related to the required competencies can be helpful. Make sure that the interviewer is aware that you have supportive documents but allow him or her to show interest in what you have.

- Be pleasant during the interview. It doesn't hurt to smile on occasion. Some candidates come to the interview looking as if that had just eaten a sour lemon. A gentle smile softens the immediate tension of the interview. Smile, on occasion, to let him or her know that you are happy to be a part of the process. **Don't over do it**. During the interview, make sure that you have good eye contact with the interviewer. Looking around or out of the window can give the impression of a lack of focus or interest. Be comfortable in your skin and refrain from invading the interviewer's space by being overly aggressive with your body language.

- Come prepared with a set of questions you may have developed as a result of your interest in the business or for clarification of information that you may received from your research. By all means do research and commit some of the information to memory. It impressive when the interviewer feels that you have really taken the process seriously. Most data can be found on the internet. Some data to consider: 1) the history of the company

2) customers and competitors 3) market and market share 4) Mission/vision statement 5) Income history/margins 6) Market cap 7) Company's pipeline of products 8) Employment levels and history. 8) Company culture 9) Job time requirements, etc.

- Upon leaving each stage of the interview process, thank the interviewer for his/her time and restate your continued interest in the position. An exchange of business cards is appropriate as it will give you the information needed to respond with a written thank you.

- Within the first week after the completion of the interview(s), send a brief note to all interviewers, via email or letter, thanking them for the opportunity. It shows class, interest and follow up skills.

Just as a final reminder, the interview is your chance to convince the interviewers of your value and to show the interview team why you are the better choice for the position. Many students/candidates go into the interview process depending too much on their grade point and forget that the true winner will be the one who is able to put in front of the interviewer, an exceptional resume, a thoughtful listener, a pleasant personality and great interviewing skills. In the process, there are two interviews taking place. First, the company is interviewing you to assess your fit to the company and culture and secondly, you are interviewing the company to assess its fit to the kind of environment that will motivate and offer the best conditions for future satisfaction and growth for you. Each party has to come to the conclusion that there is a fit.

Now you have submitted an impressive resume, have passed the initial phone screen and are feeling good about the process. The call, which you have been desperately waiting for, has finally become a reality. The purpose of the call is to schedule a face to face interview. Now is when the rubber truly meets the road and you are finally in the game. All of the things that you have worked for are on the verge of being put to the test. No longer are we in a dry run situation, the true test of your preparation is becoming a reality. Go and get it! It's yours for the taking.

CHAPTER V

ARRIVAL AT THE NEW LOCATION

> *"If you play it safe in life, you've decided that you don't want to grow any more".*
>
> —*Shirley Mount Hufstedler*

Now that you have successfully convinced the company that you are their choice, what now? I will assume that you have had a successful negotiation for your salary package. Feel free to negotiate to a point but know your limits. There are many who would like to replace you in your new chair so don't be unrealistic about your requests during the process.

The first thirty days of a new job is critical to the long term success of the career endeavor. Critical points such as where you key clients and internal customers are located, meeting rooms, human resources, compensation, benefits, legal, finance, clinics, and communications channels are a must. In addition to these most important points on the check list, it's critical that you meet one on one with all of your direct reports if applicable or meet with key clients if not in a managerial position. The easier and more seamless the transition to this new environment the better the chances are that there will be a good match with the company and culture. Usually, your schedule and responsibilities will cause you to need the above listed services on an on going basis.

If you are a member of a minority group, try to find internal and external support groups that can share key culturistic information such as local cultural cuisine, barber/beauty shops, churches, social events, schools, etc. An excellent source of this information is well established affinity networks which are usually well versed on the diversity of the operation. Though this comment is applicable to anyone in a new position, I emphasize it to minority candidates specifically those going into areas where their culture is a small percentage of the total population.

An additional recommended early activity is to schedule tours of the surrounding areas. Within the first thirty days it is also a recommendation that individuals, in a managerial role, arrange through employee relations, a new manager assimilation process where the new leader has an opportunity to learn more about the new team and have them learn more about the new manager and his or her style. This process allows the new leader to learn in a very short time what would normally take several months to accomplish. In summary, the key things that individuals need to concern themselves with as they negotiate new horizons are the six P's discussed earlier: Persona, Packaging, Positioning, Presentation, Promotion and most of all Passion.

It is always is always advisable that new individual contributors or managers seek out a "buddy" to show them the basics and to answer their immediate questions.

CHAPTER VI

UNDERSTANDING THE CULTURE

> *"The hatred you're carrying is a live coal in your heart – far more damaging to yourself than to them".*
>
> —*Lawana Blackwell*

Each new environment has its own unique characteristics that have to be understood if the new employee is to effectively integrate into its culture. Companies like IBM, GE, Microsoft, Dell and Amgen are examples of companies carrying their own unique cultures and characteristics. The individual who quickly adjust to the new culture has a better chance of success than those who choose to push against it. Though cultures define companies and increase the company's ability to recruit top candidates, those same cultures will become obsolete if they don't bend and flex with the changing tide of the workplace. Because most workplaces are becoming more and more a mobile and global entity, the culture becomes as shifting sand and requires individuals who are flexible and willing to deal with ambiguity and significant change.

In order to understand what culture is within any organization, it must be defined. Culture refers to the cumulative deposit of knowledge, experience, beliefs, values, attitudes, meanings, hierarchies, religion, notions of time, roles, spatial relations, concepts of the universe, and material objects and possessions acquired by a group of people in the course of generations through individual and group striving. That's a mouth full but it is what it is. What a company respects in its employees becomes its culture. Most companies have a set of values and attributes that drive expected behavior.

So you see that this word culture is all encompassing and can sometime be difficult to unravel. Many companies create cultural norms such as specialized dress code, flex work schedules, core hours, job pooling, formalized social networks, etc. These descriptive will become cultural icons and does establish a gate for others coming into the culture to be measured against. These can also be effective recruiting tools because the environment is a key consideration for individuals seeking the right culture for new or continued employment.

Cultural norms often are so strongly ingrained in a company's culture that new employees may be unaware of certain expected behaviors. Until these behaviors are seen in the context of having some form of flexibility, they will more likely prevent certain resources from becoming a part. Often, the company may have difficulty recognizing the need for change and eventually creates tension, paralysis to a point of disengagement and job dissatisfaction. Leaders who don't value learning the cultural norms of an organization can make it more difficult for individuals to assimilate themselves to the new environment. What motivates and energize someone from an Asian background may be totally different from someone of African or European decent. Learning and understanding these differences can be the catalyst for a more productive and innovative work environment.

CHAPTER VI

UNDERSTANDING WHAT IS EXPECTED

> *"The success of any entity is predicated on its having the ability to be agile, fluid and flexible. The workforce is constantly changing and the organization that realizes that fact and act positively with a diverse mindset will be the ultimate winners. We are entering a period where the baby boomers are retiring taking with them vast stables of knowledge and expertise that will be lost if we fail to realize the importance of closing the generation gaps through participation, communication and mentorship".*
>
> —Ted Bagley

In any corporate environment, there are factors that must be understood if one is to succeed in such a competitive environment.

Time requirement – Does the company expect that individuals come in early and leave late as a visual commitment to its ideals? Does the company require frequent weekend schedules? Get an understanding of time requirements/demands during the interview process. How much travel is involved if any? The primary expectation of any company is that each individual do what is required to get the job done. There are times when weekend obligations are a must and it must be made clear, when accepting the position, that you will be flexible enough to do what is necessary within limits to accomplish the job requirements. Making your skills available to the company as needed is definitely one element of the success equation. Companies which allow employee time flexibility normally will benefit by the employee doing what is necessary to make up the time either through evening commitments or starting early. Employees with excellent work ethic, commitment, clarity of role, trust and vision…always find a way to get the job done.

Job ratings – Does the company have an employee rating system? If so, are there requirements to maintain a certain rating to advance in the company succession system? Ask questions about the rating system and understand how it can possible affect your future growth in the company. Where are the bottom and top ends of the success equation? Ask questions concerning how the rating system affects, if at all, the compensation system. In most companies, your annual rating is your ticket to the big dance. When there is a key opportunity in an area, the first things considered are the rating of the individual, competency to the posted requirements and where they are on the succession chart if applicable. Your overall success can rise or fall on your understanding the rating system.

Mobility – Mobility is defined as the flexibility to move anywhere within the company where your specific skills and services are required. Is mobility a requirement in order to progress in the company? Does a foreign assignment increase an individual's ability to move within the company? In many major companies, it's virtually impossible to be considered "high potential" if you are not willing to go where the company needs you. Many young people severely limit their careers by refusing to move to certain areas of the country.

Certainly, a company will understand the need to delay a move because of emergency situations, family requirements or educational needs but the delay should be temporary or risk derailing the progress of otherwise high potential talent. The fact that the company is willing to invest in certain types of assignment is a signal of your value or potential and should be taken advantage of.

The average international assignment, if on an expatriate status, can cost a company in the neighborhood of one million dollar per year per person. It that doesn't get your attention, nothing will. There are several messages that the company is sending. (1 that you and your skill sets are appreciated and your efforts are such that they are willing to invest in your future (2 they see your future as being bright for the company and worthy of this type financial commitment. The company will benefit in the future from these type development decisions. (3 There is a retention play here and they want to show you that they value you for the long haul.

Project Management – Does developing project management skills increase the ability of an individual to move up in the organization? Why certainly it does. In any profession, it is expected that top talent has the ability move a project from idea to implementation through sound strategy, organizational and talent deployment, time management, data story boarding and effective presentation. If there is an area where new entries tend to struggle with, it's having the skills and confidence to lead other through a process of "Idea to implementation". It requires skill, competencies, courage, courtesy, drive, candor, organization, listening, strategic planning, cooperation, time management, and above all, strong interpersonal skill to get others to follow. Now you can see why it's such a difficult area and not suited to everyone's competency level.

Presentation – How important is it to make effective presentation as a key tool in your development tool box? I say it's vital. Whenever you are presenting in any venue, you are on stage and the audience is your critic. Sometimes leaders will tell you that what they are most concerned about is the information on your slides and not your presentation style. This sometimes disarms a presenter to the point of being too casual in your presentation. That's why "always start by wearing a suit to an interview" is an appropriate piece of advice. You may be over dressed but it plays much better than being under dressed. Always remember that the first impression is definitely a lasting one. You will hear that phrase many times throughout my work because it's vital as a reminder of what's at stake. Always be at your absolute best when presenting. You never know who is listening. Always do a dry run of your presentation with others who are constructive critics.

In my opinion, effective presentation is an art, not a science. Some have it and some don't. Some will learn it and some won't. It is a critical part of the success equation.

Strategic Skills – It is highly recommended that while in college or in early career mode, the strategic mental process development skills are fine tuned to develop a total business perspective, business acumen and client based competency level. Those in B school usually have the opportunity to test these skills before embarking on their career destination. This involves learning to deal in an environment of ambiguity, action orientation and business politics. These strategic skills also require strategic agility, the ability to move and change directions at a moment's notice based on business direction and need. Being able o anticipate future consequences and act prior to impact instead of fighting the fire after it's consumed a lot of time resources and energy.

Courage – The ability to analyze, coach and direct in a highly competitive work environment where creativity is a key ingredient in whether you succeed or fail. This involves the "how to" of conflict management, confronting difficult situations, and calming the waters where turbulent discussions have need for closure. Courage allows one to build effective teams, manage and measure work, drive for results and set priorities. How one copes with change, act responsibly and handle risk and uncertainty goes a long way in establishing the corporate courage needed in dynamic environments.

Political Savvy – Being able to view corporate politics as necessary and a key part of corporate life. This takes time and experience in order to maneuver through and around complex situations with the minimal amount of business disruptions. Political savvy is a part of knowing how the team and the organization functions in good and bad times. It requires knowing ones personal strengths, weaknesses, opportunities and realities and knowing when to look beyond those things that are obvious.

CHAPTER VII
THINGS THAT ARE CAREER BOOSTERS

"The best way to predict the future is to create it."

—*Abraham Lincoln*

There are always those individual career tid-bits that it's always good to know. It sometimes gives you just a step ahead of the crowd. Consider these:

- Develop a <u>network</u> of people who you can call on and <u>count on</u> both within and outside of your area of responsibility. Also make sure that that favor is returned. Be more than willing to step out of your <u>comfort zone</u> when adding tools to your career toolbox. Being comfortable is like treading water, you are staying afloat but you are not going anywhere. Always leave an employer better than you found them because there may be a need to return.

- Don't be afraid to <u>stretch yourself</u> to higher limits by taking assignments that pushes your competencies to their limit. Failure is not a death sentence unless it becomes a habit.

- <u>Volunteer</u> to lead or support projects outside your normal scope of responsibilities. It's called career courage. Those that have it are leading major corporations today. Be sure to add value during your tenure because value translated into job security.

- <u>Understand and value diversity</u> within your work space, it will pay dividends. Diversity should be inclusive not exclusive. We tend to be afraid of things we know little about. Those that see diversity as "accepting less than", is like an ostrich with its head in the sand. It may be blind to the impending situation but leaves its flank exposed as other can and will take advantage. It is a proven fact that a diverse workforce is more productive. The accumulation of data from many different sources and backgrounds increases the richness of the data outcome.

- Keep external issues to a minimum which tends to decreases the internal pressures. The <u>less stress</u> you bring to work decreases that which you will encounter during the normal day. Know that people are always looking at you either positively or negatively based on their interaction with you or their perception of you.

- How you <u>start</u> a career has much to do with how you <u>finish</u>. Also the means of your career will justify the extremes.

- Turn your <u>shortcomings</u> into <u>opportunities</u>. We tend to learn twice as much from our mistakes than from our successes. Show me someone who has not made a mistake and I will show you a person that lacks the creative gene.

- <u>Stay calm</u> in the face of adversity although it's easier said than done. <u>Adversity</u> is the thing that tries each of our souls and it measures those who are capable of staying in the game.

- Stay current with your <u>competencies</u> because each year the bar is raised on performance. Each year, whether you realize it or not, you have to re-interview for your position because in most companies, the stakes are high and only the best will stand the test.

- Don't be afraid to <u>test your assumptions</u>, some will be winners and some won't. Don't be afraid of curiosity

- Don't just <u>let things happen</u>…<u>make them happen</u>. Someone else is depending on you more than you know.

- Organized your life, thoughts, work and your desk. Clutter can be habit forming.

- The saying that <u>attitude</u> does affect <u>aptitude</u> which intern affects <u>altitude</u> is right on the money. Your personality and behavior is the screen door to your brand.

- Identify several mentors along life's highway. They are there primarily to remind us that the solution to most of our problems is within us.

- Listen more than you talk. When you do speak…have something of substance to say. Talking too much leaves less time for listening.

- Every relationship developed is a potential opportunity. Make sure that each contact each day is as positive as you can make them. Positive encounters breed strong resource networks.

- Minimize the surprises to your leader or the work group based on your actions. You can never have too much communication with the decision makers.

CHAPTER VIII
THE VALUE OF MENTORING/COACHING

"The greatest good you can do for another is not just to share your riches but to reveal to him his own".

—*Benjamine Disraeli*

No matter how strong a performer one may be, it is advisable early in your career to have a coach or mentor that is experienced in giving advice on career direction and development needs. Having someone who is knowledgeable about your area of expertise, key leadership traits as well as having knowledge of the company and its key strategies and direction can be a major asset.

First, selecting the appropriate mentor is critical to the success of the union. Many mentees choose mentors for the wrong reason. They seek individuals who are in significant positions in the company but who may or may not have time to invest in their development. These mentors are there in name only and in many cases does not have the best interest of the mentee as one of their primary initiatives. Many mentors are assigned as a part of some formalized program that the company has developed usually targeting either minorities, females or hi potential employees. Companies also make the mistake of sometime developing mentor programs strictly for minorities and or females. The unintended message in that action is that the groups are somehow flawed and need special attention in order to succeed in a select environment. If that is not the intent, then open the opportunity for anyone needing mentors and not specify race or gender.

One of the best descriptions of the value of a mentor came from Susan Vitale who wrote an article for HRO Today Magazine. She stated that, "When you have the right mentor in the workplace, your chance of succeeding has improved. One of the greatest, most valuable benefit of a mentor can be summed up in one word: experience. We have to understand that these experienced resources have traveled these familiar roads and many can benefit from their wisdom. A mentor can help you decide when it is time to take the next step in your career as well as help you devise a strategy to do so. A good mentor can help you assess your skills and identify what your strengths and weaknesses are".

Companies sometimes tend to make the mistake of matching women with other women or minorities with other minorities. A good mentorship is based on chemistry and not necessarily based on race, gender or job classification. Usually, more effective mentors are outside the mentees work group but understand the challenges within it. They tend to be less affected by the internal politics and will give candid and uncut advice where internal mentors can't help being affected by the internal political climate. That doesn't say that internal mentors are ineffective. Sometimes it depends on their individual mentor and their position within the organization.

Another key point to consider is that many of these mentors may be competent in their areas of responsibility but doesn't have the skills or desire required to be an effective mentor or counselor.

Most effective mentor/mentee relationships happen unexpectedly. The chemistry develops automatically and the relationship is unplanned. A true mentor receives tremendous satisfaction observing the transformation of their clients from usually insecure raw talent to confident top talent within the organizational structure. The successful mentor /mentee relationship takes time and effort on the part of each participant.

The mentor, if truly invested in the relationship, will set aside a minimum of one hour per month for a face to face meeting. He/she would chart the course of the relationship by establishing initial ground rules for the meetings and always starting with an agenda. Effective and experienced mentors are rare. Because of the quality and time requirements, an effective mentor should not maintain more than three mentees at a given time.

Things to share with the mentor are:

- Your current appraisal (if applicable.)
- Any individual development initiative
- Current performance rating
- Any documents listing development needs.
- Long term aspirations
- Fears and reservations concerning the job.
- Resume showing last 5 years of development
- Current individual/manager relationship perception.
- How you are perceived by others either through documented feedback like the 360 degree process or other data collection devices.

The mentor will request a resume, appraisals, job description, and any other document to assist is the orientation of the mentee. Next comes the face to face initial session to establish the expectation of both sides. Once expectations are satisfied, a meeting schedule is established and the mentorship is activated. The length of the mentorship depends mainly on time required to reach the agreed upon goal. Formal Mentor/mentee programs are successful also where there is good chemistry, a wiliness to give of the time and a healthy desire to a successful outcome.

Mentor/mentee relationships can change over time. A mentee can conceivably move to a point in the relationship with their competencies where their current mentor can no longer assist in their growth and a new mentee is required to continue the positive trend. This is a normal transition of career growth and is not an indication of the effectiveness of the current mentor. It is very important that the correct transition timing is realized.

The mentor is "not the manager" and should be very careful not to create tension in the relationship between the individual and the manager by suggesting actions that are counter to the instructions of the leader. A good mentor will, at the appropriate time, make know to the leader the presence of the mentorship and act as a positive contributor to the overall relationship. There will be times when the mentor is at odds with the leader's direction and must be careful not to cause the relationship between the leader and employee to deteriorate. A good mentor will keep the leader abreast of the development trends

CHAPTER IX

PERSONAL BRANDING

> *"All of us need to understand the importance of branding. We are CEOs of our own companies: Me Inc. To be in business today, our most important job is to be head marketer for the brand called <u>You</u>."*
>
> —*Tom Peters*

In order to be an effective sales person, one must know their product in painful detail; have confidence in their ability to persuade; be genuine in their presentation and have strong negotiating skills. Earlier in this book I mentioned "Branding". What is it and why is it important?

A brand is a name, term, design, symbol or any other identifying characteristic that identifies you, your product or a service. On a ranch, cows and horses were branded with a hot iron specifying that they were owned by that rancher. It also signified the quality of the heard. Certain brands bring a higher beef price at the market. Proper branding can result in more exposure and greater opportunity for an individual or organization. If your brand carries a positive history, it opens doors for you that may be closed to other having a lesser brand. Brands are typically made up of various characteristics:

- Name – Once you have a track record of accomplishment, your name is labeled with success and the ability to achieve. This success can come in the form of grades, projects, presentation or job accomplishment.

- Executive Presence – Many individuals command attention when they enter a room, others do by leaving. This attention usually is characterized by individuals having a command of speech, dress, and personality. Some have this presence, some don't. Some will have it at some point of the career life cycle, and some want.

- Ability – Looking the part is short lived if there is no substance, competence or record of accomplishment. You must not only talk the talk, you must walk the walk. A dressed up pig is still a pig. In other words, looking the part is part of the equation but the substance behind the look gets to the brand.

- Influencing skills – Having the ability to rally others around ideas, vision and direction. Without these influencing characteristics, it becomes virtually impossible to drive the team concept.

- Personality – Your personality opens up many opportunities that may not exist to others having a more introverted nature. Personality is the particular combination of emotional, attitudinal, and behavioral response patterns of an individual having a profound effect on others.

- Diversity mindset- Having the ability to embrace those of other cultures and value that difference through team dynamics and mentoring opportunities.

The Benefit of Branding

1. Increased Marketability –A great brand will cause other employers to look for you rather than you looking for them.
2. Image of accomplishment – Project management skills
3. Economic upside to compensation – Increased compensation and long term incentives.
4. International exposure and expatriate opportunities – Global exposure to expanding markets.
5. Exposure to stretch assignments – Company willing to invest in your future personal growth.

Many individuals are unemployed today because they have a tarnished brand and don't know how to correct it. What companies see is more of the same so that want take the chance. Your brand can be refreshed by seeking new skills and competencies. Here is a check list for you to consider if you feel as if your brand needs an overhaul:

1. What behaviors do you display? Are you warm, easy to approach, confident, comfortable in your own skin?
2. When was the last time you refreshed your competency tool kit?
3. How are your communication skills both written and verbal?
4. Check your wardrobe, is an update in order? Clothes doesn't make the person but it's definitely a clue to the kind of person you are. Inappropriate appearance can be a significant turn off.
5. What organizations are you affiliated with. It can be a clue to the depth and breadth of one's experience.
6. What certifications do you hold in your area of expertise?
7. Are you associated in any way with the community? Do you volunteer ?
8. Do you seek others feedback on your performance/image?
9. How often do you calibrate and test your Brand for leaks?

This is just a check list to see how functional your brand is. The whole idea of personal branding suggests that success comes from self-*packaging*. As new entrants to the workforce, your packaging and your work ethic are primary drivers to your ability to reach another rung on the career ladder. Being productive becomes a habit and so does being none productive. Leading edge companies are not dictators of time but treat their employees in a way that has a trust element to it. Treat people like adults and they respond like adults. Treat them like children and they respond in a similar manner. Tell individuals what's expected of them and what they can expect and they will in most cases react and respond positively. Companies loose valuable productivity and dedication because of the lack of trust.

According to a Gallup, a Washington based Organization who keep close ties with data related to productivity and other measures, only 30% of U.S. workers are engaged in their work, and the ratio of actively disengaged to engaged employees is more than 2-to-1, meaning the remaining 70% are stopping short of their full potential – a problem that has significant implications for the economy and the individual of American companies.

SUMMARY

> *"Always bear in mind that your own resolution to succeed is more important than any other".*
>
> —*Abraham Lincoln*

"Colin Powel once said," The less you associate with some people, the more your life will improve. Any time you tolerate mediocrity in others, it increases your mediocrity. An important attribute in successful people is their impatience with negative thinking and negative acting people. As you grow, your associates will change. Some of your friends will not want you to go on. They will want you to stay where they are. Friends that don't help you climb will want you to crawl. Your friends will stretch your vision or choke your dream. Those that don't increase you will eventually decrease you. Never receive counsel from unproductive people. Never discuss your problems with someone incapable of contributing to the solution, because those who never succeed themselves are always first to tell you how.

No truer words have ever been spoken. There are those in your life that you need to shed, get rid of because they are no more than leaches who drain the last blood from you before moving on to the next host. They scheme, plot, lie cheat and steal to keep your attention and when you least expect it, they tarnish your brand for simply being in their company. That's a hard call because many of these people are so called friends that you grew up with.

You are the potential leaders of the new millennium. Do you accept that responsibility or fear it? Do you have what it will take to lead corporations and businesses into the future? Companies are constantly seeking individuals who can unequivocally answer these questions without hesitation. The demands of business are surely redefining our leadership expectations and direction. Companies are quickly defining who are in the categories of top talent and key to retain. Those fitting that label according to some statistics are as few as 30-35 percent of any high performing organization. Leaders of the future, I contend, will be defined as those who have presence that others are willing to follow because of their vision, personality, competence and savvy. They will be able to lead high performing teams with a diverse characteristic. They must have character and integrity so that when they speak other will buy into their direction. Once trust is an issue, leaders turn to managers and failure is the usual result. Broken trust is a deep hole that you id difficult to get out of. Good leaders always develop a solid road map to their destination. They surround themselves with talent that exceeds their own capabilities. They have excellent judgment when assessing business direction and mission. They are flexible enough to change direction when data tells them to do so. Leaders like Steve Jobs, past CEO of Microsoft, Michael Dell, CEO of Dell Computer, Bob Bradway, CEO of Amgen, are excellent role models of these traits. These leaders hold their organizations accountable for living the values of the business as well as creating solid leadership attributes to govern themselves and the organization.

It's a proven fact that most corporate attrition can be tracked to poor leadership, a faulty culture, lack of opportunity and unfair treatment. Many poor leaders ignore their development need or blind spots and tend to try to solve their problems through counseling or coaching. A major change in behavior is usually not experiences until the individual recognizes the problem as real. Most leaders who are given this feedback will punch the card but not seek real change opportunities because they feel that others have the problem and not them. Many noted companies are moving away from flexible work arrangements according to many studies because companies don't trust that people can manage themselves and remain productive.

According to reports by Workforce magazine, 77 percent of the surveyed companies allow telecommuting and 60 percent of their career growth because of "out of sight, out of mind". Flex work arrangements came about in the 90's when there was the computer boom.

COMMANDMENTS OF KEEPING YOUR JOB
(Texas Business today 1998)

- Be on time, whether it is with showing up for work, returning from a meeting or even a schedule one on one discussion. Being late effects your time and the time of the other individual. It also gives a glimpse of your dependability or self-order.

- Executives believe that telecommuting is not productive and hampers breaks, going to meetings, or turning in assignments. Your success is predicated on your productivity whether in line of sight or not. You may not think people are watching your actions, but they are. Telecommuting, remote work assignments and working basically away from the mother ship is a growing trend that will continue.

- Call in if you know you will be tardy or absent. Most companies treat absences or tardiness without notice much more seriously than simple absence or tardiness. Unless you are incapacitated, make the call yourself. It gives more credibility to your situation.

- Try your best; always finish an assignment, no matter how much you would rather be doing something else. It is always good to have something to show for the time you have spent.

If you are unable to complete an assignment in the committed window of time, communicate it in a timely manner and not wait until the project due date is upon you.

- Anticipate problems and needs of management - your bosses will be grateful, even if they do not show it. Don't just identify problems…come up with possible solutions.

- Show a positive attitude - no one wants to be around someone who is a "downer". Your behavior, in many instances, will dictate how others on the team act or react.

- Avoid backstabbing, office gossip, and spreading rumors - remember, what goes around comes around - joining in the office gossip may seem like the easy thing to do, but almost everyone has much more respect - and *trust* - for people who do not spread stories around. Often, this is a symptom of an individual who has trust issues. They thrive on controversy and get their energy from "DIRT".

- Follow the rules. The rules are there to give the greatest number of people the best chance of working together well and getting the job done. Just make sure that the rules are updated and are current to the ever-changing environment.

- Look for opportunities to serve customers and help coworkers. Those who would be leaders must learn how to serve. Good leaders sometimes in their lives were good at following. Remember the old saying, "the customer is the key".

- Avoid the impulse to criticize your boss or the company. It is easy to find things wrong with others - it is much harder, but more rewarding, to find constructive ways to deal with problems. Employees who are known for their good attitude and helpful suggestions are the ones most often remembered at performance evaluation and raise review time. Look for ways to work with even those who are difficult personalities. Maybe your influence from a positive standpoint, can rub off on them.

- Volunteer for training and new assignments. Take a close look at people in your organization who are "moving up" - chances are, they are the ones who have shown themselves in the past to be willing to do undesirable assignments or take on new duties. Ask yourself, "What are they doing they I am not". People tend to gravitate around winners. Are you a winner?

- Avoid the temptation to criticize your company, coworkers, or customers on the Internet. Social networking sites like Facebook, MySpace, Twitter, and blogs offer many opportunities to spout off – remember that anyone in the world can find what you put online and that employers may be able to take action against any employee whose online actions hurt the company or its business in some way.

- Be a good team member. Constantly focusing on what makes you different from others, instead of how you fit into the company team, makes you look like someone who puts themselves first, instead of the customer, the team, or the company.

- Try to avoid ever saying "that's not my job". Many, if not most, managers earned their positions by doing work turned down by coworkers who were in the habit of saying that, and they appreciate employees who help get the job done, whatever it is. Do whatever it takes, within laws and reason, to get the job done.

- Show pride in yourself and respect toward others. Never let yourself be heard uttering minority-related slurs or other derogatory terms in reference to yourself or to others. Use of such terms perpetuates undesirable stereotypes and inevitably disturbs others. It also tends to make others doubt your maturity and competence. The best way to get respect is to show respect toward yourself and others.

- Distinguish yourself. Pick out one or more things in your job to do better than anyone else. Become known as the "go-to" person for such things. That will help managers remember you favorably at times when you really need to be remembered.

- Have excellent written and verbal communications skills. Being able to express yourself in front of a group, within a team or on paper is a major plus to your personal brand.

A FINAL NOTE

You are about to venture out into a world that is unforgiving, one that does see the color of your skin before it sees the content of your character; One where constant mistakes can cost time, money and sometimes your career. It's a world where politics, scandals, job loss, foreclosures, broken homes and war get much too much publicity over things like education, Christianity, family values and ethics.

Sometimes, it just seems that no matter how much you try to do.... it's **just not enough**. In the news, no matter what happens positively, the media gives it a negative spin.....We had the two young women released from prison in South Korea but they criticized the motive; the economy is starting to change for the positive, but there is still criticism that the President is **not doing enough**. It is up to you as new potential leaders to change that disturbing trend. It's not about politics, it's about knowledge and education.

As new entrants in the workforce, you have a right to be proud of what you have accomplished, you are a part of only an average of 70% of students across the country who graduates from college. In comparison, there are millions of students who drop out sometimes during the 4 years. I don't plan to pepper you with a lot of statistics but statistics are our frame of measurements of success or failure. In California, the high school drop-out rate is 20% or 1 in 4 children.

This is the last of my stats, I promise. The graduation Rate for California by race is as follows:

Asian	92.9%
White	75.7%
Hispanic	57.0%
Black	55.3%
American Indian	49.7%

Some you will disagree with me and that's ok but I at least hope you keep an open mind to what I am saying. Some of my words will fall on stony ground and die a natural death, but some hopefully will fall on good rich mental dirt and will stay with you for a long time and the trunk of your tree of life will grow strong and sturdy.

The question I have for all of you is "now that you have gotten this far, what now? You have made the initial commitment to excellence but what now?

As a nation, our primary concern for all of our resources should be not whether they set their goals to high and fall short….our concern should be whether they set their goals too low and accomplish them.

Some of us older heads remember our parents challenging us to soar with the eagles because the air is fresh up there and there is little clutter…..or they would say keep your feet on the ground like chickens but you are constantly stepping in mess.

I am talking to our future leaders right now….whether you like it or not. You can choose to lead or be lead. To lead means that you have a degree of control, to be lead means that you are under the control of others. Now don't get it twisted, it's ok to be lead as long AS YOU ARE CAPABLE OF LEADING.

Candidates, listen to me good……You can only get out of this life what you put into it. These are tough and changing times so it's imperative that you put on your full armor.

You can't afford to have your head or feet exposed to the elements until you are ready for them to be. The buck does not stop here, you are just scratching life's surface. Success comes before work only in the dictionary.

It will not be enough for you to be the best at what you do….you must be better than the best.

A widely known preacher once preached a sermon entitled "hitchhikers in the road of glory". His point, one which I think to be appropriate is that some of us go through life as "users" only. We never get involved in anything unless we can get a profit from it. Like scavengers we live off the toils and labors of others. But, But these type people who refuse to pull their weight are never happy. They live and die and when they are gone, the world barely notices.

It is possible to have a neutral effect on the world. A neutral person is neither hot nor cold, they are lukewarm. Food taste good either hot or cold but there is something about lukewarm stuff that just doesn't set right with me.

Lukewarm people are just like that; they are always scheming and stretching the truth. You all know people like that, they will change their positions or their minds at a moment's notice. They always say what they think people want to hear. One day they are on one side and the next day they are on the other. I call these folks windshield wipers. They are usually well liked but seldom respected. They are popular but not trustworthy. Don't be lukewarm in your careers.

As I finish this summary, if you don't remember anything else that I said in this book, try to remember this. Success is a verb not a noun. A noun just sits there and waits for something like an adjective or adverb to modify it. A verb is an action word; it makes things happen in a sentence. Without the verb, the sentence is dead and has no meaning. Without you being an active participant in your career aspirations, you are a noun and I refuse to modify you. I don't want you all to wind up as a dangling participle. UH-UH, I may have lost some of you right there. How quickly we forget our Basic English lessons.

The only one that can hold you back is you. It's time to find out just who you are, what you want, where you are going and how you are going to get there. The rules as you know them will continually change; roadblocks will not only be in your path but sometimes intentionally placed there simply to test your metal.

It matters not that you get knocked down in this life, it matters that you pick yourself up, brush yourself off and get back in the game. I love to quote from some of our great leaders from the past like Fredrick Douglass. He said, "If there is no struggle, there is no progress. Those who propose to favor freedom and yet depreciate agitation are men who want crops without plowing the ground. They want rain without thunder and lightning. They want the oceans' majestic waves without the awful roar of its waters."

I said that I wouldn't be long so I want to honor that promise but let me leave these principals for you:

ABOUT THE AUTHOR

Please indulge me as I attempt this daunting task or penetrate too far into this malaise of information on becoming successful, it is sometimes most important to share with my readers a little about me so that each of you can determine whether I am, in your mind, qualified to address this topic. Briefly, I was educated at Ullman High School in Birmingham Alabama. That hallowed ground, where our principal George Bell ruled the property with an iron fist, has now given way to the massive University of Alabama Medical Center. That piece of ground was destined to produce some of the greatest minds in the country either through the educational process or the medical mainstream. It produced some of the brightest clinical brains that is today the foundation of human therapeutics and clinical research which continues to drive leading edge ideas to increased generational longevity. That hallowed ground laid the foundation for many of our lawyers, doctors and business minds who are now a part of the boomer generation.

I completed my undergraduate work at Ohio State University and Franklin Business Law School in Columbus Ohio. I continued my education at North Carolina Central University, in Durham North Carolina where I received my Masters Degree in Psychological and Educational Counseling. My true education to life came in the military through the Presidential Honor Guard or the Old Guard as it was often called, in Ft. Myers Virginia. At Ft. Myer, I had the honor of standing security watch over the eternal flame at the grave site of one of our great President of these United States of America, John F. Kennedy. I was also assigned as a member of the honor guard's firing party that supported the burial of soldiers killed in battle primarily during the Vietnam conflict. Vietnam was the point where my life changed forever.

After the escalation of the Vietnam War in the 60's, many of us, in that prestigious unit called the Old Guard, were asked to serve on the battlefields in Southeast Asia. The war years were challenging as well as life altering. After receiving the Bronze star medal of valor for meritorious service in battle, I finished my military service and proceeded to complete my degree in Business Administration at Franklin Business Law School. Upon completing my college experience, my work life included the following companies: The General Electric; Russell Athletics; Dell Computer, and currently Amgen Pharmaceuticals where I hold the position of Vice President Human Resources for its Global Operations Division. Over thirty years of my career was spent in Human Resources, the genesis of my knowledge on the subject. I continue to serve on community boards like the Moorpark Foundation; Big Brother and Big Sister Presidents Council and just recently joined the board of the gold Coast Veterans Foundation. I also serve on the Board of Directors for my beloved fraternity, Kappa Alpha Psi, Inc.

Hopefully that gives you some degree of comfort that I have dabbled around in this subject a bit and have the experience and wisdom to have shared my knowledge on the subject. To have accomplished as much as I have, means that I have not only been through many interviews but I have observed many young people entering the work world with no clue of the environment and what lay ahead as they plow head first into the swift currents of Corporate America.

NOTABLE QUOTES

"In Prosperity Our Friends Know Us. In Adversity We Know Our friends."

"Never make someone a priority when you are only an option for them."

"If you are going to achieve excellence in big things, you develop the habit in little matters.

Excellence is not an exception, it is a prevailing attitude..".

—Colin Powel

Opportunity is missed by most people because it is dressed in overalls and looks like work.

—Thomas A. Edison

Success is not measured by what you accomplish, but by the opposition you have encountered, and the courage with which you have maintained the struggle against overwhelming odds.

—Orison Swett Marden

Do not go where the path may lead, go instead where there is no path and leave a trail.

—Ralph Waldo Emerson

Everyone who has ever taken a shower has had an idea. It's the person who gets out of the shower, dries off, and does something about it that makes a difference.

—Nalan Bushnell

Entrepreneurs are simply those who understand that there is a ittle difference between obstacle and opportunity and are able to turn both to their advantage.

—Niccoa Machiavelli

I hear and I forget. I see and I remember. I do and I understand,

—Confucius

If I have seen further than others, it is by standing upon the shoulders of giants.

—Isaac Newton

REFERENCES

Lair, Daniel J.; Sullivan, Katie; Cheney, George (2005). "Marketization and the Recasting of the Professional Self". *Management Communication Quarterly*

Ernest & Young. "2007 Aging U.S. Workforce Survey: Challenges and Responsibilities - An Ongoing Review.

Human Resource Executive. "The Age factor. New Strategies and Resources for Senior Human Resources Executives.LRP Publications.

HRO Today: Recognition, *Is your workforce in focus*, July/August edition. Optimizing Workforce Operations.

www.ingramcontent.com/pod-product-compliance
Lightning Source LLC
LaVergne TN
LVHW041624070526
838199LV00052B/3237